muffins

muffins

IRRESISTIBLE CREATIONS TO SHARE WITH FAMILY AND FRIENDS

75 RECIPES SHOWN STEP BY STEP IN 300 BEAUTIFUL PHOTOGRAPHS

CAROL PASTOR

LORENZ BOOKS

This edition is published by Lorenz Books
an imprint of Anness Publishing Ltd
Hermes House, 88–89 Blackfriars Road
London SE1 8HA
tel. 020 7401 2077; fax 020 7633 9499

www.lorenzbooks.com; www.annesspublishing.com

If you like the images in this book and would like
to investigate using them for publishing, promotions
or advertising, please visit our website
www.practicalpictures.com for more information.

UK agent: The Manning Partnership Ltd
sales@manning-partnership.co.uk

UK distributor: Book Trade Services
uksales@booktradeservices.com
exportsales@booktradeservices.com

North American agent/distributor: National Book Network
www.nbnbooks.com

Australian agent/distributor: Pan Macmillan Australia
customer.service@macmillan.com.au

New Zealand agent/distributor: David Bateman Ltd
tel. (09) 415 7664; fax (09) 415 8892

Publisher: Joanna Lorenz
Editorial Director: Helen Sudell
Editor: Simona Hill
Photographer: Charlie Richards and Craig Robertson
Stylists: Liz Hippisley and Helen Trent
Designer: Simon Daley
Proofreading manager: Lindsay Zamponi
Editorial Reader: Penelope Goodare
Production Controller: Christine Ni

ETHICAL TRADING POLICY

Because of our ongoing ecological investment programme,
you, as our customer, can have the pleasure and reassurance
of knowing that a tree is being cultivated on your behalf to
naturally replace the materials used to make the book you
are holding. For further information about this scheme, go to
www.annesspublishing.com/trees

COOK'S NOTES

• Bracketed terms are intended for American readers.
• For all recipes, quantities are given in both metric and
imperial measures and, where appropriate, in standard cups
and spoons. Follow one set, but not a mixture, because they
are not interchangeable.
• Standard spoon and cup measures are level. 1 tsp = 5ml,
1 tbsp = 15ml, 1 cup = 250ml/8fl oz.
• Australian standard tablespoons are 20ml. Australian
readers should use 3 tsp in place of 1 tbsp for measuring
small quantities.
• The nutritional analysis given for each recipe is calculated per
cake. If the recipe gives a range, such as Makes 8–9, then the
nutritional analysis will be for the smaller size, i.e. 9 cakes.
Optional ingredients and those added 'to taste' are not included.
• Large (US extra large) eggs are used unless otherwise stated.

Main front cover image shows Lemon and elderflower poppy
seed muffin (see page 52).

PUBLISHER'S NOTE

Although the advice and information in this book are believed
to be accurate and true at the time of going to press, neither
the authors nor the publisher can accept any legal responsibility
or liability for any errors or omissions that may be made nor
for any inaccuracies nor for any harm or injury that comes
about from following instructions or advice in this book.

Contents

Introduction

The muffin has become a modern-day culinary phenomenon. Baked in an individual muffin tin and with a distinct cup shape and golden domed top, the muffin can be filled with sweet or savoury ingredients, and have a light or dense texture.

Two types of muffin are popular today – the English muffin, an individual round, flat bread, made of dough, baked on a griddle, and often served toasted and spread with butter, and the American muffin, an individual cake, usually sweet, baked in the oven. English and American muffins are distinct from each other in taste and texture, and apart from in name are unlikely ever to be confused. American muffins originated as small baked breads, but with the introduction of new raising agents in the mid-19th century, and the addition of a wider range of ingredients in recent decades, they have evolved to become more cake-like. American muffins differ from cupcakes too, although the distinctions between the two are becoming less clear. In its early form, a muffin would have been made with different grains giving it a heavier texture, whereas a cupcake is baked with flour and is almost always sweet with a characteristic decorative frosting.

The earliest American muffins were known as corn dabs and originated in the southern United States. They were baked in heavy iron gem pans with lozenge-shaped

moulds using the corn harvested from the vast prairies. Maize was combined with pearl ash, a raising agent, and with sour milk or buttermilk, to make the muffins rise. They were delicious served as a hot side dish with stews and chilli. Sweeter versions were made with nuts, raisins, dried fruits, apples and blueberries. Maple syrup, with its light smoky flavour, was a common sweetener in the mid-19th century. The muffin became so popular that a dry mix was later adapted that could be kept in the refrigerator for several weeks at a time without going off. It was mixed in huge quantites and passed around family and friends to take a share.

HOW MUFFINS ARE MADE

The muffin is now as familiar as the sponge cake. The 'muffin method' of baking, though, is quite different to that used for other baked goods. Muffins are made in two stages: the dry ingredients (flour, sugar, dried fruit, nuts and so on) are mixed together in one bowl and the wet (eggs, oil or melted butter) in another. The two are mixed together long enough to dampen the flour with as few strokes as possible. The art is not to overmix the batter, leaving small pockets of floury clumps in the mixture. The result is a batch of muffins that are light in texture and well risen. Over-worked batter can produce heavy muffins.

HOLDING THE BATTER

A large quantity of muffin batter may need to be baked in several batches, meaning that some batter may be held back for 30 minutes to an hour or so. Holding the batter will not spoil the appearance or texture of the muffins (unlike traditional cakes). If you partly stir 20–25ml/ 1½ tbsp of flour through the held-back batter just before baking it will cause the crowns to split when baked, which can be an attractive feature.

READY-TO-BAKE MUFFIN MIXES

A home-made, ready-prepared muffin mix to use at a moment's notice makes good sense, if you like to eat muffins. The dry Canadian muffin mix recipe (see

Left Savoury corn muffins made with a traditional recipe. Their domed top is a distinct feature of classic muffins.

page 14) provided can be prepared in large or small quantities and stored in an airtight container in the refrigerator for up to one month. Just add eggs and buttermilk to activate the raising agent.

Store freshly baked muffins, without their toppings, in airtight containers for up to three or four days. Muffins can be frozen at this stage. Defrost at room temperature. Once decorated with frosting, the muffins should be eaten quickly or stored in the refrigerator overnight.

BAKING TINS AND MOULDS

Muffin batter may be added directly to lightly greased muffin tins (pans), or the muffin tin can be lined with paper cases. A little smear of butter at the base of each of the holes will secure the cases and make it easier to fill them. Paper cases are useful in two ways: they keep the pans cleaner and the muffins fresher for longer.

A mini muffin paper case measures 3.5cm/1½in in diameter. A standard muffin paper case measures 6.5cm/2½in in diameter and a large muffin paper case measures 9cm/3½in in diameter. Tall muffins are baked in dariole moulds and contain the same amount of batter as a large muffin paper case.

OVENS AND BAKING MUFFINS

Remember that ovens do vary in terms of the temperatures that they reach and where it is best to position the batter within the oven. These factors can make the difference between a perfectly baked muffin and a slightly overdone one, so use a thermometer to test the temperature of your oven before baking anything. The recipe timings that follow and the descriptions of baked colour and texture are given as a guide. However, the best indicator of when a muffin is baked is that the centre bounces back when lightly pressed. A skewer inserted into the centre should come out clean.

Right Chocolate muffins made with cocoa and chunks of chocolate are great for an occasional treat.

Above Mixing the wet ingredients together in one bowl, then adding them to the combined dry ingredients, gives muffins a light texture. Luxury ingredients are added last.

MUFFINS FOR EVERY OCCASION

Versatile and practical, there are muffins in this book to suit every occasion. They are perfect for breakfast when filled with nutritious oats and dried fruits, or for packing in a lunch box with an apple and a carton of fruit juice. When lavishly decorated with thick swirls of candy frostings, the sweet and indulgent recipes are delicious for special treats. Left plain, or drizzled with syrup, a fruit-packed muffin is a great pick-me-up for any time of day. Mini muffins filled with vegetables make delightful savoury appetizers or accompaniments that are the perfect side dish to soups and salads.

Ingredients

A muffin can be made from relatively few ingredients, but the addition of fruit, oats, chocolate, herbs and spices or even savoury products such as bacon and cheese will transform a humble cake into something much more appealing.

Alcohol The alcohol content of any drink you add will evaporate during baking, leaving a luxurious flavour. Calvados (apple brandy) enhances muffins made with pears, apples, or quince. Amaretto (almond-flavoured liqueur) adds to the flavour of peach almond and apricot muffins. Marsala (fortified wine) has a special affinity with pears, chocolate and coffee. *Crème de cassis* (blackcurrant liqueur) is perfect for blackcurrant muffins. Sloe gin and white rum are also used.

Baking powder When mixed into batters this chemical leavener produces carbon dioxide, which makes tiny bubbles. During baking the bubbles expand and the mixture sets, adding volume and lightening the texture. Baking powder is double acting, which means that it begins to form the carbon dioxide when combined with liquid and continues to do so when baking.

Below Buttermilk, eggs, flour, sugar and butter are the ingredients needed to make a basic sweet muffin.

Bran Made from the outer layer of cereal, such as the husks of wheat or oats, bran is a natural product valued for its fibre content. It adds flavour and texture to muffins.

Butter and oil Salted butter is used unless stated otherwise. For dietary reasons vegetable oil may be used as a substitute for butter. Other oils including olive, corn and sunflower are also used.

Buttermilk Low in fat and slightly sour to taste, buttermilk is the liquid left after butter has been churned. Its sourness activates the raising agent in the cake batter.

Cheese French Brie and soft herb and garlic cheese add a light tart flavour to savoury recipes. Cheddar, Parmesan and Stilton each add a strong, robust flavour.

Below Bran, maple syrup, yogurt, oats, sultanas (golden raisins), cranberries and ready-to-eat dried apricots are some of the ingredients used to transform a basic muffin into a breakfast treat.

Chocolate Dark chocolate, which contains 70 per cent cocoa solids, is generally the best chocolate to use for baking. Its slightly bitter and intense chocolate flavour is not easily overshadowed by the other ingredients. Plain (semisweet) chocolate is a good choice for those who prefer a less bitter taste. White chocolate adds sweetness to muffins.

Condensed milk is a skimmed milk that is condensed by various stages of boiling until it is thick and creamy with a delicious sticky texture. To enrich it further the cans may be boiled in a pan of boiling water for several hours to produce a dense amber-coloured caramel, known as *dulce de leche* (also available ready-made.)

Cornmeal (polenta) Made from ground corn, the texture of cornmeal can be coarse or fine. Choose finely ground.

Below Fresh berries and other soft fruits add appealing flavour and texture to sweet muffins.

Crème fraîche The delicate sourness of crème fraîche contrasts well with warm melted chocolate for a delicious cake topping.

Eggs Large (US extra large) eggs are used in the recipes in this book unless otherwise stated.

Flavourings Concentrated fruit juice, or fruit drinks intended to be diluted, add flavour to frosting or syrup. Almond and vanilla extracts add intense flavour. For a coffee flavour, instant coffee granules can be diluted with a few teaspoons of hot water, but a double strength of your favourite fresh coffee is best.

Flour Different flours affect the texture and flavour of muffins as well as affecting the raising agent. Plain (all-purpose) flour is a soft, white wheat flour that has no raising agent (baking powder) added. Self-raising (self-rising) flour is the same with the addition of a raising agent. Barleycorn flour is cream-coloured and made from wheat and barley flours combined with malted barley flakes and linseed. It adds flavour, texture and fibre to muffins. Spelt

Below Vegetables and herbs may not appear to be likely muffin ingredients, but many work well together.

flour is pale beige with a light, flavoursome wheat or nutty flavour. Light rye flour is a pale beige flour that adds a strong distinctive flavour. Some recipes use a mix of flours to add different flavours.

Fruit Use fresh fruit when it is in season, because out-of-season fruits often have less taste. Sharp-tasting berries such as blackcurrants or cranberries may be partly cooked in the oven first with sugar and butter before they are added to the muffin batter. Mandarins or clementines can be boiled and puréed (skin and all) to make distinctive, zesty muffins. Dates (fresh or dried), raisins, prunes, sultanas (golden raisins) and dried apricots are frequently used in batters. Freshly squeezed juice, grated rind and quince paste also add flavour.

Herbs and spices Parsley, thyme, oregano, rosemary and garlic add aroma and flavour to baking. Chop all herbs finely before you add them to the recipe. Commonly used spices include cinnamon, ginger, nutmeg and mixed (apple pie) spice.

Below Dulce de leche, marshmallows, chocolate and nuts are just a few of the indulgent ingredients used to make decadent, show-stopping muffins.

Maple syrup is graded according to colour and strength of flavour. Like honey it can be used in place of sugar to add sweetness to muffins.

Nuts and seeds Chopped or ground, nuts add a distinctive flavour and a crunchy texture to muffins. Caraway and sesame seeds add a delicious taste.

Sugar Soft light brown sugar has a light caramel flavour. Soft dark brown sugar has a strong, smoky and slightly bitter flavour. Unrefined brown sugars have the best flavour. Caster (superfine) sugar is the best to use for muffins made using the creaming method because the crystals dissolve quickly. Icing (confectioners') sugar is used for making frostings.

Vegetables make versatile ingredients in muffins and should be finely grated before they are added to the batter. Use courgettes (zucchini), marrow (large zucchini), pumpkin, squash, onions, carrots, beetroot (beet) and sweet potato for sweet and savoury flavours.

Below Bacon, cheese, dates and mushrooms and are just a few of the ingredients that can be added to savoury muffins. Dates add sweetness.

Baking kit

Although it is possible to make do with a few multi-purpose kitchen utensils, it is better to invest in quality equipment if you intend to bake muffins on a regular basis. A good selection of different moulds, cutters and interesting paper liners will add an extra dimension to your muffins.

Baking parchment This can be used for lining the muffin tins (pans) or terracotta pots, or for cutting little paper collars for the muffins after baking.

Baking tins A small shallow baking tin is required in some of the recipes for baking fruit with sugar and jam.

Decorative cookie cutters These are available in all shapes and sizes for making decorations to top muffins. Choose metal rather than plastic cutters for well-defined shapes. Decorative cutters can be purchased from specialist cookware shops, but you may find a larger selection if you search the internet.

Electric food mixer For time-saving and convenience, electric food mixers are great for beating together butter and sugar, and for beating eggs. However, it is advisable to fold in the dry ingredients by hand. Some mixers have a liquidizer attachment – useful for making fruit purées.

Electric whisk A light hand-held whisk is ideal for making buttercream and for whipping cream.

Flowerpots Small, heat-resistant terracotta flowerpots, available from good kitchenware shops (rather than those from garden centres, which have a drainage hole in the base), make attractive baking containers. Make sure to grease them well before you add the lining paper, or you may have trouble releasing the muffins from the mould.

Grater A box cheese grater is perfect for grating hard cheese as well as a variety of vegetables. Grated chocolate is also used in one or two of the recipes. For best results, chill the chocolate overnight in the refrigerator before you grate it.

Kitchen scissors Keep scissors in your working area and use them specifically for culinary purposes, such as snipping bacon and fresh herbs into muffin batters and, of course, cutting paper liners.

Left Weighing scales, a measuring jug (cup), balloon whisk, a wire rack, measuring spoons, fine whisk, wooden spoon, sieve (strainer), mixing bowls and a cheese grater are basics.

Left Standard muffin trays, large muffin cups, individual dariole moulds, terracotta pots and small cake tins (pans) are all used to make muffins in this book.

Knives A palette knife is useful for smoothing buttercream and frostings over the tops of cakes and muffins. A sharp-pointed knife is useful for cutting shapes around paper templates when cutting from cookie dough.

Measuring cups and jugs Level off the top of each filled cup with the back of a knife for an accurate quantity of a dry mix ingredient. Do not interchange metric and imperial measurements while baking.

Mixing bowls Small, medium and large mixing bowls are all useful for different stages of muffin making. A set of small bowls is handy for small quantities of ingredients, or for separating eggs.

Muffin tins (pans) These are available in tin or silicone materials. The muffin cups may have sloping sides, which are wider at the top than at the bottom, or they may be slightly taller with straight sides. Muffins baked in either shape of tin use the same paper cases and take the same amount of time to bake. Individual dariole moulds are used to make tall, slim muffins.

Ovenproof china cups These make unusual baking receptacles for muffins. They are available from specialist cookware shops. Choose medium-sized cups with a 175ml/6fl oz/¾ cup capacity, which is the perfect size to line with a standard paper case. Alternatively, china cups make an attractive holder in which to present muffins in paper cases.

Paper cases The finely pleated muffin cases are convenient for easy release, help to keep muffins fresher for longer, and mean less washing up of sticky tins for the cook. In the absence of a muffin tin treble the paper cases (one inserted inside the other) and bake the muffins free-standing on a baking sheet in the oven. Dariole moulds or tall, slim muffin tins are lined with pleated cake cases cut to size from paper liners used for loaf tins.

Pastry brushes These are available from good kitchenware shops and supermarkets. Choose one that looks like a small, flat decorator's brush, if you have a choice.

Piping (pastry) bags For piping buttercreams and other creamy frostings; large piping bags are usually made from fabric and fitted with large plastic nozzles that can easily be washed, dried and reused. Ready-made, disposable piping bags made of baking parchment are used for piping thin lines for small decorations. Snip off the merest tip of the bag for an instant nozzle.

Sieves (strainers) Use a sieve for sifting flours with raising agents, or for sifting out any lumps from icing (confectioners') sugar. Use a tea strainer to sift coffee granules.

Spoons Exact spoon measurements are vital. Dry ingredients should be levelled off the spoon with a knife. A large metal spoon is efficient for folding in dry and wet ingredients, without losing air from the batter. Use a wooden spoon for beating.

Weighing scales Invest in a set of scales to weigh precise quantities. Use either imperial or metric measurements, never a combination.

Basic sweet muffin

A basic sweet batter can be enhanced with many different flavours, but fresh fruit is the simplest. Raspberries are used here but you could try fresh apricots, blueberries, blackcurrants or figs, cut into bitesize pieces. Serve warm, lightly dusted with icing (confectioners') sugar, if you like.

MAKES 7–8 STANDARD MUFFINS

For the basic sweet muffin
225g/8oz/2 cups plain
   (all-purpose) flour
12.5ml/2 rounded tsp
   baking powder
150g/5oz/³/₄ cup golden caster
   (superfine) sugar
75g/3oz/6 tbsp butter, melted
2.5ml/½ tsp vanilla extract
1 egg, lightly beaten
200ml/7fl oz/scant 1 cup
   buttermilk

For flavouring
150g/5oz/scant 1 cup raspberries
15ml/1 tbsp caster (superfine)
   sugar (optional)

1 Preheat the oven to 180°C/350°F/
Gas 4.

2 Lightly grease the cups of a muffin tin (pan) or line them with paper cases.

3 If you are using berries that are too tart for your taste, arrange the fruit in a single layer on a plate and sprinkle with 15ml/1 tbsp sugar. Set aside.

4 To make the batter, sift the dry ingredients into a mixing bowl and form a well in the centre.

5 In a separate bowl, mix the melted butter, vanilla extract, egg and buttermilk together. Pour into the dry ingredients then fold partly together.

6 Lightly combine half of the fruit and any syrup into the batter. Spoon the mixture into the prepared paper cases and sprinkle the remaining fruit on top.

7 Bake the muffins for 25 minutes, until they look golden and well risen and are springy to the touch.

8 Leave to cool and set slightly in the tin, then transfer them from the tin to a wire rack to cool further. Serve fresh, or allow to go cold and store in an airtight container for up to 3 days.

Energy 261kcal/1101kJ; Protein 4.7g; Carbohydrate 43.6g, of which sugars 22.1g; Fat 8.9g, of which saturates 5.4g; Cholesterol 46mg; Calcium 89mg; Fibre 1.3g; Sodium 95mg.

Basic savoury muffin

This basic recipe has many variations. Here a soft herb cream cheese and buttermilk are the basis for the 'savoury' flavour, while bacon adds extra saltiness. Eat savoury muffins fresh for the best flavour. Store in an airtight container for up to three days.

MAKES 7 LARGE MUFFINS

For the basic savoury muffin
225g/8oz/2 cups self-raising
  (self-rising) flour
10ml/2 tsp baking powder
10ml/2 tsp maple syrup or caster
  (superfine) sugar
1 egg
75g/3oz/6 tbsp butter, melted
115g/4oz/½ cup soft garlic and
  herb cream cheese
175ml/6fl oz/¾ cup buttermilk

For flavouring
30ml/2 tbsp olive oil, for frying
15g/½oz/1 tbsp butter, for frying
225g/8oz very lean smoked bacon,
  plus extra to serve
maple syrup, to serve

1 Preheat the oven to 180°C/350°F/ Gas 4. Line the cups of a muffin tin (pan) with paper cases.

2 Sift the flour, baking powder and sugar, but not the maple syrup, into a bowl. Make a well in the centre.

3 Beat the egg, butter, cream cheese and buttermilk together in a bowl with the maple syrup, if using.

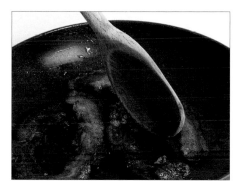

4 In a frying pan, heat the oil and butter over a medium heat and fry all the bacon, until it is lightly caramelized, about 4 minutes. Remove from the heat. Cut the bacon into tiny pieces and set aside a small quantity for serving.

5 Pour the wet ingredients into the well in the dry ingredients.

6 Add the bacon and any juices from the pan. Mix until combined.

7 Spoon the batter into the paper cases and bake for 25–30 minutes, until the muffins are golden.

8 Leave to cool slightly, then serve warm, topped with extra bacon. Drizzle over warm maple syrup.

Energy 395kcal/1644kJ; Protein 10.5g; Carbohydrate 27g, of which sugars 3.2g; Fat 28g, of which saturates 14.6g; Cholesterol 90mg; Calcium 167mg; Fibre 1g; Sodium 790mg.

Canadian muffin mix

A mix of semi-prepared ingredients can be kept in an airtight container in the refrigerator, ready to make muffins. You need one quantity of basic dry mix, and one quantity of wet ingredients. The flavourings can vary. Eat fresh for best taste, or store in an airtight container for three days.

MAKES 16 STANDARD MUFFINS

For the basic dry mix
450g/1lb/4 cups plain
  (all-purpose) flour
175g/6oz/³/₄ cup butter, diced
30ml/2 tbsp baking powder
pinch of salt
275g/10oz/1¹/₃ cups caster
  (superfine) sugar

For flavouring
75g/3oz/³/₄ cup pecans,
  roughly chopped
rind of 1 large orange, finely grated
50g/2oz/4 tbsp sesame seeds
275g/10oz/1¹/₃ cups dried
  mixed berries

For the wet ingredients
4 eggs
400ml/14fl oz/1⅔ cups buttermilk

Pecan and berry mix

1 Sift the flour into a large mixing bowl. Add the butter and rub it into the flour to form very fine breadcrumbs. Ensure that the butter has a long shelf-life.

2 Sift the baking powder, salt and sugar into the flour and butter mixture, then add the flavouring ingredients. Stir well to combine the ingredients evenly.

3 Transfer the contents to an airtight container and store in the refrigerator for up to 1 month.

4 Preheat the oven to 180°C/350°F/ Gas 4. As a change from paper cases, cut baking parchment into 12.5cm/ 5in squares and press into the greased cups of a muffin tin (pan).

5 Decant the dry muffin mix into a mixing bowl. Stir in the wet ingredients, until just combined.

6 Spoon the batter into the paper cases until almost full and bake for 25 minutes, until a skewer inserted into the centre comes out clean.

7 Leave to stand and set in the tin for a few minutes before turning out on to a wire rack to go cold.

Energy 368kcal/1546kJ; Protein 6.6g; Carbohydrate 53g, of which sugars 31.5g; Fat 15.9g, of which saturates 6.9g; Cholesterol 74mg; Calcium 127mg; Fibre 1.7g; Sodium 118mg.

CALCULATING QUANTITIES

• For 8 muffins weigh half of the basic dry mix and flavouring (650g/1½lb) into a mixing bowl. Mix lightly with 2 eggs and 200ml/7fl oz/scant 1 cup buttermilk.

• For 4 muffins weigh a quarter of the quantity of basic dry mix (350g/12oz) and flavouring into a mixing bowl. Mix lightly with 1 egg and 100ml/3½fl oz/scant ½ cup buttermilk.

• For 2 muffins weigh 175g/6oz of the basic dry mix and flavouring into a mixing bowl. Mix lightly with ½ egg and 50ml/2fl oz/¼ cup buttermilk. Spoon the batter into paper cases and bake for 25 minutes until risen and cooked through.

Pear muffin for two variation

Make a muffin in a 12.5cm/5in cake tin (pan). Make up the batter using half the basic dry mix and half the wet ingredients. Substitute the dried fruit with a peeled (and cored) pear, half of it chopped and incorporated and the other half placed on top of the batter.

Dried apricot muffins variation

Use one quantity of basic dry mix and one quantity of wet ingredients. For flavouring, in place of the dried mixed berries substitute the same quantity of chopped ready-to-eat dried apricots. Make up the batter as for the Canadian muffin mix.

Walnut and pecan muffin variation

Mini flowerpots are not only for gardeners. Heat-resistant terracotta pots are available in cookware shops for baking bread and can also be used for muffins. Make sure to line them well. Use one quantity of basic dry mix and one quantity of wet ingredients. Substitute the dried mixed berries for 365g/13oz/3¼ cups mixed walnuts and pecans, finely chopped. Make up the batter as for the Canadian muffin mix.

Blueberry muffin variation

The perfect breakfast treat is a blueberry muffin baked in an ovenproof coffee cup. Choose a 175ml/6fl oz/¾ cup capacity cup and line it with a large paper case. Use the Canadian muffin mix and in place of the dried berries use the same quantity of fresh blueberries. Serve warm for breakfast with a drizzle of maple syrup, if you like, and your favourite fresh ground coffee.

Indulgent toppings

Many muffin recipes are devised to be eaten unadorned straight from the paper case, while others are plainer in content and ideal for topping with luxurious buttercreams, fruity jams, warm and buttery sauces, dried fruit crisps, and soft and sweet marshmallows.

Pink raspberry buttercream

Perfect for raspberry or plain buttermilk muffins.

MAKES ENOUGH TO COAT 8 MUFFINS

175g/6oz/³/₄ cup butter, softened
350g/12oz/3 cups icing (confectioners') sugar, sifted
20ml/4tsp lemon juice
25ml/1½ tbsp raspberry jam, sieved (strained)
1 or 2 drops red food colouring (optional)

1 In a large bowl, beat the butter with the icing sugar until smooth and fluffy. Stir in the lemon juice and sieved jam.

2 Add a few drops of food colouring and stir until the buttercream is evenly coloured and a soft consistency.

Passion fruit and lime curd

Eat with warm citrus muffins and serve with yogurt.

MAKES 450G/1LB

30ml/2 tbsp juice and grated rind of 1 lime
115g/4oz/½ cup butter
175g/6oz/³/₄ cup caster (superfine) sugar
1 egg, plus 3 yolks
3–4 passion fruit, flesh sieved (strained)

1 Put the lime juice and rind, butter and sugar in a medium pan. Lightly beat the egg with the egg yolks and add to the pan.

2 Add the passion fruit. Stir over a medium heat until thick. Pour into a glass jar. Seal. Chill for up to 1 month.

Energy 2734kcal/11466kJ; Protein 2.8g; Carbohydrate 383g, of which sugars 383g; Fat 143g, of which saturates 94.5g; Cholesterol 403mg; Calcium 218mg; Fibre 0g; Sodium 1338mg.
Energy 2037kcal/8516kJ; Protein 33.9g; Carbohydrate 222g, of which sugars 222g; Fat 118.7g, of which saturates 69g; Cholesterol 1060mg; Calcium 283mg; Fibre 22.3g; Sodium 1098mg.

Oven-dried pear and apple crisps

Caramelized oven-dried fruit slices add a natural and appealing decoration to fresh fruit muffins.

MAKES 16 CRISPS

1–1½ small ripe, firm pears, unpeeled and thinly sliced
1–1½ small ripe apples, unpeeled and thinly sliced
115g/4oz/generous ½ cup caster (superfine) sugar

1 Line a baking sheet with parchment. Preheat the oven to 120°C/250°F/Gas ½. Arrange the fruit slices between sheets of kitchen paper to drain off their juices.

2 Put the sugar and 100ml/3½fl oz/scant ½ cup water in a pan. Heat gently until the sugar dissolves and bring slowly to the boil. Leave to boil briskly for 3 minutes, then remove from the heat.

3 Pour the syrup into a bowl and immerse the fruit in it for 2–3 minutes. Remove the fruit (reserving the syrup) and spread out the slices over the baking sheet.

4 Bake for 2–2½ hours until the slices shrink and turn crisp. Leave to dry over a wire rack in a warm place. Brush with cooking syrup before serving. Store in a cool, dry place interleaved in silicone paper for up to 1 month.

Quick blueberry jam

Spoon blueberry jam and plain (natural) yogurt over blueberry or berry brioche muffins, or a recipe with spices, apples or nuts. This delicious jam also adds a sweet note to more substantial healthy bran muffins.

MAKES 450G/1LB

350g/12oz/3 cups blueberries
200g/7oz/1 cup caster (superfine) sugar
thin 5cm/2in strip of lemon peel

1 Put the blueberries in a heavy pan with 50ml/ 2fl oz/¼ cup water. Bring to the boil, then simmer for 5 minutes, until the berries burst, stirring occasionally.

2 Add the sugar and lemon peel, then stir in gently and continue to stir until the sugar dissolves. Boil for 7 minutes, or until the jam thickens, stirring occasionally.

3 Pour the hot jam into clean, sterilized and warmed glass jars. Seal and leave to go cold. Store in the refrigerator for up to 1 month.

Energy 67kcal/286kJ; Protein 0.2g; Carbohydrate 17.6g, of which sugars 17.6g; Fat 0g, of which saturates 0g; Cholesterol 0mg; Calcium 10mg; Fibre 0.6g; Sodium 2mg.

Energy 987kcal/4197kJ; Protein 4.5g; Carbohydrate 258g, of which sugars 244g; Fat 0g, of which saturates 0g; Cholesterol 0mg; Calcium 106mg; Fibre 7g; Sodium 12mg.

Warm caramel sauce

This sauce keeps in a covered bowl in the refrigerator. Warm it through before using it to regain its flowing consistency.

MAKES ENOUGH TO COAT 8 MUFFINS

275g/10oz/1½ cups caster (superfine) sugar
150ml/10 tbsp crème fraîche or double (heavy) cream

1 Put the sugar in a pan with 150ml/10 tbsp water and simmer gently over a medium heat, stirring continuously until dissolved. Bring to the boil until it turns golden.

2 Remove from the heat and plunge the base of the pan in a bowl of cold water for a few seconds to arrest the cooking.

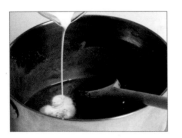

3 Stir in the cream. If the caramel stiffens, replace the pan over a low to medium heat and stir until it is smooth and glossy. Serve warm, or reheat gently if necessary.

4 Allow to go cold before refrigerating for up to 1 week in a sealed container.

Chocolate, toffee and mascarpone cream

The sweet combination of caramel and mascarpone is offset by the intense bitterness of the chocolate.

MAKES ENOUGH TO COAT 9 MUFFINS

225g/8oz dark (bittersweet) chocolate,
  broken into pieces
30ml/2 tbsp warm caramel sauce (see left)
250g/9oz/1⅓ cups mascarpone
15ml/1 tbsp Marsala (optional)
5ml/1 tsp vanilla extract (optional)
chocolate-covered coffee beans (optional)

1 Put the chocolate in a heatproof bowl over a pan of gently simmering water. When the chocolate melts remove from the heat and stir in the warm caramel sauce.

2 Gradually beat in the mascarpone until the chocolate cream is smooth, glossy and evenly coloured. Mix in the Marsala and/or the vanilla extract, if using.

3 Spread on the muffins, and top with coffee beans.

Energy 875kcal/3689kJ; Protein 2.4g; Carbohydrate 158.6g, of which sugars 158.3g; Fat 30g, of which saturates 20.3g; Cholesterol 85mg; Calcium 123mg; Fibre 0g; Sodium 26mg.

Energy 1745kcal/7293kJ; Protein 33.9g; Carbohydrate 174.7g, of which sugars 162.7g; Fat 105.9g, of which saturates 63.5g; Cholesterol 137mg; Calcium 102mg; Fibre 0g; Sodium 28mg.

Marshmallows

This confection, with its soft texture, is perfect for topping muffins for children.

MAKES 98

50g/2oz/¹/₂ cup icing
   (confectioners') sugar, sifted
50g/2oz/¹/₂ cup cornflour
   (cornstarch), sifted
225g/8oz/generous 1 cup sugar
15ml/1 tbsp glucose syrup
9 sheets leaf gelatine
5ml/1 tsp vanilla extract
2 egg whites

1 Lightly oil a shallow baking tin (pan) 30 x 20 x 2.5cm (12 x 8 x 1in). Dust it with half of the icing sugar and cornflour, sifted together, to evenly coat the base.

2 Place the sugar, glucose syrup and 200ml/7fl oz/scant 1 cup water in a pan and bring slowly to the boil, stirring frequently until the sugar dissolves. Boil rapidly until the sugar thermometer reaches 127°C/260°F.

3 Soak the leaf gelatine in 150ml/ ¼ pint/⅔ cup cold water and set aside for 10 minutes, then melt the gelatine, in a pan, in its soaking water over a low heat.

4 Pour the leaf gelatine liquid into the sugar syrup. Stir twice. Pour into a metal bowl. Stir in the vanilla.

5 Place the egg whites in a bowl and whisk into stiff peaks. Continue whisking and pour in the syrup in a slow, thin stream. It will gradually start to thicken to the stiff peak stage. When all the syrup is added continue to beat for another 10 minutes until thick and glossy.

6 Pour into the prepared tin and smooth the surface with a wet knife.

7 Chill for 1 hour. Cut into squares and dust with the remaining icing sugar and cornflour mixture. Store between sheets of silicone paper in an airtight container.

VARIATIONS
Add colour and flavourings at the end of step 5, if you like.
• For deep rose, add 3–4ml/ ³/₄ tsp rose water, plus a few drops red food colouring.
• For chocolate add 3–4ml/ ³/₄ tsp chocolate extract plus enough unsweetened cocoa powder to colour.
• For blueberry add 3–4ml/ ³/₄ tsp blueberry extract and a few drops of violet food colour.

Energy 1335kcal/5696kJ; Protein 5.1g; Carbohydrate 350.1g, of which sugars 317.3g; Fat 0.2g, of which saturates 0g; Cholesterol 0mg; Calcium 165mg; Fibre 0g; Sodium 132mg.

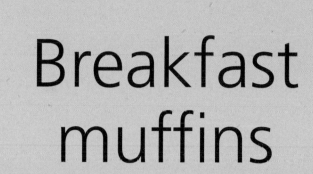

Breakfast muffins

Warm muffins, fresh from the oven, may be a breakfast
treat to be reserved for weekends or special occasions,
but when made with nutritious and sustaining
ingredients, they make the ultimate convenience food.
This delightful recipe collection is packed with familiar
breakfast fare – toasted oats and bran, honey and
marmalade, lightly spiced fresh and dried fruits,
and chopped nuts and yogurt. With a pot of strong tea
or espresso coffee they make a ritual to savour. Try
berry brioche muffins split open and spread with butter
and a spoonful of dark berry preserve, or spiced
sultana muffins, densely packed with dried fruits. For a
healthier choice, muffins made with bran make an
excellent start to the day, or for a more decadent
indulgence try rhubarb muffins with ginger topping.

Honey and yogurt muffins

These filling and substantial wholemeal breakfast muffins are sweetened with honey rather than with sugar, so are not overly sweet. Different flavours of honey will give a subtly different taste to these muffins, so try a few varieties to see which you prefer.

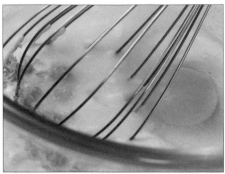

3 In a bowl, whisk together the yogurt, egg, lemon rind and juice. Add the butter and honey mixture. Set aside.

MAKES 12 STANDARD MUFFINS

55g/2oz/¼ cup butter
75ml/5 tbsp clear honey
250ml/8fl oz/1 cup natural
   (plain) yogurt
1 egg
grated rind of 1 lemon
65ml/2fl oz lemon juice
150g/5oz/1¼ cups plain
   (all-purpose) flour
175g/6oz/1½ cups wholemeal
   (whole-wheat) flour
7.5ml/1½ tsp bicarbonate of soda
   (baking soda)
pinch of freshly grated nutmeg

1 Preheat the oven to 190°C/375°F/ Gas 5. Line the cups of a muffin tin (pan) with paper cases.

2 In a small pan, melt the butter and honey over a gentle heat. Stir to combine. Remove from the heat and set aside to cool slightly.

4 In another bowl, sift together the dry ingredients.

5 Fold the dry ingredients into the yogurt mixture to blend, then fill the prepared cups two-thirds full.

6 Bake until the tops spring back when touched lightly. This should be around 20–25 minutes.

7 Leave to cool in the tin for 5 minutes before turning out on to a wire rack. Serve warm or at room temperature, drizzled with honey, if you like. Store the cold muffins in an airtight container for up to 3 days.

Energy 155kcal/652kJ; Protein 4.7g; Carbohydrate 25.4g, of which sugars 6.9g; Fat 4.6g, of which saturates 2.5g; Cholesterol 25mg; Calcium 66mg; Fibre 1.7g; Sodium 50mg.

Banana and raisin muffins

Sweet and full of flavour, these muffins are sure to be a breakfast favourite. Bananas are the ultimate in providing food fuel that will keep you feeling fuller for longer. Raisins add sweetness and, like bananas, are full of nutritional value.

MAKES 10 STANDARD MUFFINS

250g/9oz/2¼ cups plain
    (all-purpose) flour
5ml/1 tsp baking powder
5ml/1 tsp bicarbonate of soda
    (baking soda)
pinch of salt
2.5ml/½ tsp ground cinnamon
pinch of grated nutmeg
3 large ripe bananas
1 egg
70g/2½ oz/5 tbsp dark brown sugar
50ml/2fl oz/¼ cup vegetable oil
30g/1oz raisins

1 Preheat the oven to 190°C/375°F/ Gas 5. Lightly grease the cups of a muffin tin (pan) or line them with paper cases.

2 Into a bowl, sift together the flour, baking powder, bicarbonate of soda, salt, cinnamon and nutmeg. Set aside.

3 Chop the bananas into another bowl. With an electric mixer, beat the peeled bananas at moderate speed until mashed.

4 Beat the egg, sugar and oil into the mashed bananas.

5 Add the dry ingredients and beat in gradually, on low speed. Mix until just blended. Stir in the raisins.

6 Fill the prepared cups two-thirds full. For even baking, half-fill any empty cups with water.

7 Bake until the tops spring back when touched lightly, around 20–25 minutes.

8 Leave in the tin to set for a few minutes. Transfer to a rack to cool. Eat when at room temperature or cold. Store in an airtight container for up to 3 days.

Energy 187kcal/788kJ; Protein 3.4g; Carbohydrate 35.8g, of which sugars 16g; Fat 4.3g, of which saturates 0.6g, Cholesterol 19mg, Calcium 45mg, Fibre 1.2g, Sodium 10mg.

Crunchy breakfast muffins

Toasted oat cereals are widely available and make a delicious and crunchy addition to these moreish muffins. The raisins add a sweetness to the light texture of this batter. Serve with strong coffee for a late breakfast or brunch.

MAKES 10 STANDARD MUFFINS

150g/5oz/1¼ cups plain
  (all-purpose) flour
7.5ml/1½ tsp baking powder
30ml/2 tbsp caster (superfine)
  sugar
250ml/8fl oz/1 cup milk
1 egg
50g/2oz/¼ cup butter, melted
200g/7oz toasted oat cereal and
  raisins mixed

1 Preheat the oven to 350°F/180°C/ Gas 4. Lightly grease the cups of a muffin tin (pan) or line them with paper cases.

2 Sift the flour into a bowl. Add the baking powder, then the sugar and stir in. Make a well in the centre.

3 In a jug (pitcher), using a fork, beat the milk with the egg and the melted butter.

4 Pour the liquid into the well in the flour mixture. Stir lightly until just combined.

5 Stir in the cereal and raisins. Bake for 20–22 minutes until risen and golden. Leave to cool in the tin for a few minutes, then turn out on to a wire rack to go completely cold. Serve fresh, or store in an airtight container for up to 3 days.

Energy 180kcal/759kJ; Protein 4.6g; Carbohydrate 29.8g, of which sugars 10.8g; Fat 5.6g, of which saturates 3.2g; Cholesterol 32mg; Calcium 68mg; Fibre 2.5g; Sodium 210mg.

Prune muffins

Sticky and full of flavour, the humble prune is low in fat, full of fibre and contains antioxidants and minerals in abundance, making it a healthy choice of dried fruit. French Agen prunes are considered the best for flavour, and here they are flavoured with grated nutmeg.

MAKES 12 STANDARD MUFFINS

1 egg
250ml/8fl oz/1 cup milk
120ml/4fl oz/½ cup vegetable oil
50g/2oz/4 tbsp caster
  (superfine) sugar
25g/1oz/2 tbsp soft dark
  brown sugar
285g/10oz/2½ cups plain
  (all-purpose) flour
10ml/2 tsp baking powder
pinch of grated nutmeg
115g/4oz cooked pitted
  prunes, chopped

1 Preheat the oven to 200°C/400°F/ Gas 6. Lightly grease the cups of a muffin tin (pan) or line them with paper cases.

2 Break the egg into a bowl and beat with a fork. Beat in the milk and oil.

3 Stir in the sugars. Set aside.

COOK'S TIPS
• Prunes are full of fibre and a well-known natural laxative.
• Store in an airtight container for up to 3 days.

4 Sift the flour, baking powder and nutmeg into a mixing bowl. Make a well in the centre, pour in the egg mixture and stir until moistened. Do not overmix; the batter should be slightly lumpy.

5 Fold in the prunes. Fill the prepared cups two-thirds full. Bake until golden brown, about 20 minutes. Let stand for 10 minutes before turning out on to a wire rack. Serve warm or at room temperature.

Energy 190kcal/801kJ; Protein 3.7g; Carbohydrate 28.1g, of which sugars 10.7g; Fat 7.8g, of which saturates 1.2g; Cholesterol 17mg; Calcium 66mg; Fibre 1.3g; Sodium 17mg.

Raisin and bran muffins

Low in fat and in sugar, these dense and filling muffins are made with a combination of wholemeal flour and bran, and are flavoured with cinnamon and raisins. The brown sugar adds caramel notes to the depth of flavour.

4 Add the bran, raisins and sugars and stir until blended.

5 In another bowl, mix together the egg, buttermilk, lemon juice and melted butter.

6 Add the buttermilk mixture to the dry ingredients and whisk lightly and quickly until just moistened. Do not overmix the batter.

MAKES 5 STANDARD MUFFINS

40g/1½oz/⅓ cup plain
  (all-purpose) flour
55g/2oz/½ cup wholemeal
  (whole-wheat) flour
7.5ml/1½ tsp bicarbonate of soda
  (baking soda)
5ml/1 tsp ground cinnamon
30g/1oz/⅓ cup bran
85g/3oz raisins
65g/2½oz/⅓ cup soft dark
  brown sugar
50g/2oz/¼ cup caster
  (superfine) sugar
1 egg, beaten
250ml/8fl oz/1 cup buttermilk
juice of ½ lemon
50g/2oz/¼ cup butter, melted

1 Preheat the oven to 200°C/400°F/ Gas 6.

2 Grease the cups of a muffin tin (pan) or line them with paper cases.

3 In a mixing bowl, sift together the flours, bicarbonate of soda and cinnamon.

7 Spoon the mixture into the prepared paper cases, filling the cups almost to the top. Half-fill any empty cups with water so that the muffins bake evenly.

8 Bake for 15–20 minutes. Let stand for 5 minutes, before turning out on to a wire rack to cool. Serve warm or at room temperature. Store in an airtight container for up to 3 days.

Energy 89kcal/374kJ; Protein 2g; Carbohydrate 13.4g, of which sugars 8.9g; Fat 3.4g, of which saturates 1.9g; Cholesterol 20mg; Calcium 34mg; Fibre 1.1g; Sodium 36mg.

Oat and raisin muffins

Rolled oats are a versatile cereal with many health-giving benefits, more often associated with porridge at breakfast time. Mixed with buttermilk, they plump up to add bulk to food, helping you to feel full for longer. They help lower cholesterol and are full of dietary fibre.

MAKES 12 STANDARD MUFFINS

85g/3oz/generous 1 cup rolled oats
250ml/8fl oz/1 cup buttermilk
120g/4oz/½ cup butter, softened
100g/3½oz/scant ½ cup soft dark
 brown sugar
1 egg
115g/4oz/1 cup plain (all-purpose)
 flour
5ml/1 tsp baking powder
2.5ml/½ tsp bicarbonate of soda
 (baking soda)
30g/1oz/3 tbsp raisins

1 In a bowl, combine the oats and buttermilk and leave to soak for 1 hour.

2 Preheat the oven to 200°C/400°F/ Gas 6. Lightly grease the cups of a muffin tin (pan) or line them with paper cases.

REPLACING BUTTERMILK
If buttermilk is not available, add 10ml/2 tsp lemon juice or vinegar to the milk. Let the mixture stand and curdle, about 30 minutes, before you prepare the rest of the muffin batter.

3 With an electric whisk, cream the butter and sugar until light and fluffy. Beat in the egg.

4 Sift the flour, baking powder and bicarbonate of soda. Stir the flour mixture into the butter mixture.

5 Add the oat mixture, then fold in the raisins. Do not overmix.

6 Two-thirds fill the paper cases. Bake for 20–25 minutes. Transfer to a wire rack to cool. Store in an airtight container for up to 3 days.

Energy 177kcal/742kJ; Protein 3g; Carbohydrate 22.3g, of which sugars 10.4g; Fat 9.1g, of which saturates 5.2g; Cholesterol 37mg; Calcium 51mg; Fibre 0.8g; Sodium 77mg.

Apricot bran muffins

These fruity muffins, packed with dried apricots and bran, are more nutritious for breakfast than a slice of toast. Packed with iron, fibre and vitamin A, dried apricots are associated with many health-giving properties. Choose organic varieties for a deeper flavour.

MAKES 12 STANDARD MUFFINS

115g/4oz/½ cup dried apricots
225g/8oz/2 cups self-raising
  (self-rising) flour
50g/2oz/½ cup wheat or
  oat bran
2.5ml/½ tsp bicarbonate of soda
  (baking soda)
30ml/2 tbsp soft light brown sugar
30ml/2 tbsp butter, melted
150g/¼ pint/⅔ cup natural
  (plain) yogurt
200ml/7fl oz/scant 1 cup milk

1 Grease the cups of a muffin tin (pan) or line them with paper cases.

2 Soak the dried apricots in a small bowl of water for 15 minutes. Roughly chop the soaked apricots into small bitesize pieces.

3 Preheat the oven to 220°C/425°F/ Gas 7.

4 In a large bowl, mix together the flour, bran, bicarbonate of soda, sugar and chopped apricots.

5 Add the melted butter, yogurt and milk to the bowl of dry ingredients. Mix lightly.

6 Two-thirds fill the prepared paper cases with batter. Bake for 15–20 minutes until a skewer inserted into the centre of one comes out clean.

7 Leave to set for 5 minutes, then turn out on to a wire rack to cool. Serve warm or eat within 2 days.

COOK'S TIP
Organic dried apricots are dark in colour because they contain no preservatives.

Energy 131kcal/553kJ; Protein 4g; Carbohydrate 23.6g, of which sugars 8.3g; Fat 3g, of which saturates 1.7g; Cholesterol 7mg; Calcium 83mg; Fibre 2.7g; Sodium 42mg.

Cherry and marmalade muffins

Bursting with fruit and a sweet, yet bitter, flavour, these muffins are topped like toast, with marmalade. Choose quality brands for the best flavour, and try different varieties, such as lime or lemon marmalade, to ring the changes.

MAKES 12 STANDARD MUFFINS

225g/8oz/2 cups self-raising
   (self-rising) flour
5ml/1 tsp mixed (apple pie) spice
85g/3oz/scant ½ cup caster
   (superfine) sugar
120g/4oz/½ cup glacé (candied)
   cherries, quartered
30ml/2 tbsp orange marmalade
150ml/¼ pint/⅔ cup milk
50g/2oz/4 tbsp butter, melted
marmalade, to glaze

1 Preheat the oven to 200°C/400°F/ Gas 6. Lightly grease the cups of a muffin tin (pan) or line them with paper cases.

2 Sift the flour into a large bowl. Add the spice.

3 Stir in the sugar and cherries.

4 Mix the marmalade with the milk and fold into the dry ingredients with the butter.

5 Spoon into the paper cases. Bake for 20–25 minutes, until golden.

6 Turn out on to a wire rack and brush the tops with warmed marmalade. Store in an airtight container for 3 days.

VARIATION
To make honey, nut and lemon muffins, substitute 30ml/2 tbsp clear honey for the orange marmalade. Instead of the glacé cherries use 50g/2oz toasted, chopped hazelnuts. Add the juice and finely grated rind of one lemon.

Energy 162kcal/686kJ; Protein 2.3g; Carbohydrate 29.8g, of which sugars 15.5g; Fat 4.6g, of which saturates 0.7g; Cholesterol 1mg; Calcium 51mg; Fibre 0.7g; Sodium 0mg.

Apple and cinnamon muffins

A classic and winning combination of ingredients, spiced apples have the most delicious aroma when they are baking. Eat these fruity muffins while they are still warm and fresh from the oven for the best flavour. Serve with coffee.

3 Add the chopped apples and mix roughly. Spoon the mixture into the prepared paper cases.

4 To make the topping, mix the crushed sugar cubes with the cinnamon. Sprinkle over the batter.

5 Bake for 30–35 minutes, until well risen and golden. Leave to stand for 5 minutes before transferring to a wire rack to cool. Serve them warm or at room temperature. Store in an airtight container for up to 3 days.

MAKES 6 STANDARD MUFFINS

1 egg, beaten
40g/1¹/₂oz/3 tbsp caster
  (superfine) sugar
120ml/4fl oz/¹/₂ cup milk
50g/2oz/¹/₄ cup butter, melted
150g/5oz/1¹/₄ cups plain
  (all-purpose) flour
7.5ml/1¹/₂ tsp baking powder
2.5ml/¹/₂ tsp ground cinnamon
2 small eating apples, peeled,
  cored and finely chopped

For the topping
12 brown sugar cubes,
  coarsely crushed
5ml/1 tsp ground cinnamon

1 Preheat the oven to 200°C/400°F/Gas 6. Line the cups of a muffin tin (pan) with paper cases.

2 Mix the egg, sugar, milk and melted butter in a large bowl. Sift in the flour, baking powder and cinnamon.

VARIATIONS
You could try other mild and sweet spices with these muffins instead of cinnamon. Mixed (apple pie) spice always works well with apples.

Energy 236kcal/995kJ; Protein 4.3g; Carbohydrate 38.2g, of which sugars 19.1g; Fat 8.5g, of which saturates 4.9g; Cholesterol 51mg; Calcium 74mg; Fibre 1.2g; Sodium 73mg.

Spiced banana muffins

Packed with soft and dense mashed banana, the addition of chopped hazelnuts provides these delightful muffins with an added crunch and the mixed spice brings depth of flavour to this breakfast treat. Rolled oats add bulk and fibre.

MAKES 12 STANDARD MUFFINS

75g/3oz/³/₄ cup wholemeal
   (whole-wheat) flour
50g/2oz/¹/₂ cup plain
   (all-purpose) flour
10ml/2 tsp baking powder
5ml/1 tsp mixed (apple pie) spice
50g/2oz/¹/₄ cup soft light
   brown sugar
50g/2oz/¹/₄ cup butter, melted
1 egg, beaten
150ml/¹/₄ pint/²/₃ cup milk
grated rind of 1 orange
1 ripe banana
20g/³/₄oz/¹/₄ cup rolled oats
20g/³/₄oz/scant ¹/₄ cup chopped
   hazelnuts

1 Preheat the oven to 200°C/400°F/ Gas 6. Line the cups of a muffin tin (pan) with paper cases.

2 Sift together both flours, the baking powder and mixed spice into a mixing bowl, then add the bran remaining in the sieve (strainer) to the bowl. Stir in the sugar.

3 Pour the melted butter into a mixing bowl. Allow to cool slightly, then beat in the egg, milk and grated orange rind.

4 Gently fold in the dry ingredients. Mash the banana, then stir it into the batter. Do not overmix it.

5 Spoon the batter into the prepared paper cases.

6 Combine the oats and hazelnuts and sprinkle a little of the mixture over each muffin.

7 Bake for 20 minutes until the muffins are well risen and golden. Leave to stand for a few minutes then transfer to a wire rack and serve warm or cold. Store in an airtight container for up to 3 days.

Energy 152kcal/642kJ; Protein 2.8g; Carbohydrate 29g, of which sugars 13.9g; Fat 3.6g, of which saturates 0.5g; Cholesterol 16mg; Calcium 34mg; Fibre 1g; Sodium 9mg.

Berry brioche muffins

A traditional sweet brioche recipe is studded with fresh blueberries and makes an unusual and luxurious muffin. For a special breakfast treat, enjoy them warm spread with blueberry or cherry jam. Prepare the brioche dough a day ahead of making the muffins.

MAKES 10 LARGE MUFFINS

15g/½oz fresh yeast
4 medium (US large) eggs
350g/12oz/3 cups plain (all-purpose) flour
50g/2oz/¼ cup caster (superfine) sugar
10g/¼oz salt
175g/6oz/¾ cup unsalted butter, softened
115g/4oz/1 cup blueberries
45ml/3 tbsp milk, for the eggwash
1 small egg yolk, for the eggwash

1 Crumble the yeast into the bowl of a food processor fitted with a dough hook. Add 10ml/2 tsp warm water and mix the two together.

2 Add the eggs, flour, sugar and salt. Beat at low speed for 6–7 minutes. Turn up to a moderate speed and gradually add the butter. Continue beating for 12–15 minutes until the dough is smooth and shiny.

3 Seal the dough in a plastic bag and chill for 24 hours, or overnight.

4 Lightly grease the cups of a muffin tin (pan).

5 On a lightly floured surface, form the dough into a flattened sausage 10cm/4in wide. Press the blueberries into the surface.

6 Cut the dough into 10 pieces. Using floured hands, form each into a ball, then press into a muffin cup.

7 Mix the milk and egg yolk in a bowl. Brush thinly over the muffins. Slash the tops twice with a knife.

8 Preheat the oven to 220°C/425°F/Gas 7. Leave the dough in a warm place to prove for 15 minutes, then bake for 13–15 minutes until golden and risen. Turn the muffins out on to a floured tray and leave to cool. Serve fresh for best results.

Energy 302kcal/1266kJ; Protein 6g; Carbohydrate 33.5g, of which sugars 7.1g; Fat 17g, of which saturates 10.2g; Cholesterol 117mg; Calcium 145mg; Fibre 1.3g; Sodium 288mg.

Rhubarb muffins with ginger

The shiny candied strips of scarlet rhubarb and paper-thin slices of stem ginger add a sweet, colourful topping to these muffins. Extra slices of stem ginger may be added to decorate the cooled muffins, if you like. Serve fresh for the best flavour, or store for up to three days.

MAKES 9–10 TALL MUFFINS

275g/10oz rhubarb, cleaned
30ml/2 tbsp syrup from a jar
  of preserved stem ginger
1 piece preserved stem ginger,
  chopped
50g/2oz/4 tbsp demerara
  (raw) sugar
150g/5oz/1¼ cups plain
  (all-purpose) flour
75g/3oz/¾ cup wholemeal
  (whole-wheat) or spelt flour
50g/2oz/¼ cup caster
  (superfine) sugar
10ml/2 tsp baking powder
2.5ml/½ tsp bicarbonate of soda
  (baking soda)
5ml/1 tsp ground ginger
120ml/4fl oz/½ cup low-fat natural
  (plain) yogurt
1 egg, lightly beaten

For the topping
15g/½oz/1 tbsp butter
15ml/1 tbsp ginger syrup
15ml/1 tbsp caster (superfine) sugar
1 piece stem ginger, finely sliced

1 Slice 175g/6oz rhubarb and put in a pan with 30ml/2 tbsp water, the ginger syrup, stem ginger and demerara sugar.

2 Bring to the boil, stirring. Lower the heat and simmer until soft, 2–3 minutes. Set aside.

3 Preheat the oven to 180°C/350°F/ Gas 4. Line the dariole moulds with tall paper cases (see page 11). Sift the dry ingredients into a bowl.

4 In another bowl, beat the yogurt and egg together. Stir in the cooked rhubarb and juices and mix into the dry ingredients. Divide the batter between the paper cases.

5 To make the topping, heat the butter, ginger syrup, 15ml/1 tbsp water and sugar in a small frying pan over a medium heat and stir until the sugar dissolves.

6 Cut the rest of the rhubarb into short fine strips and lightly stir them in the syrup. Leave to soften for 2 minutes, then add the stem ginger slices until warmed through. Remove from the heat. Add in small piles to the centre of the muffin tops and bake for 20 minutes until golden.

Energy 152kcal/646kJ; Protein 3.9g; Carbohydrate 31.1g, of which sugars 15g; Fat 2.3g, of which saturates 1.1g; Cholesterol 23mg; Calcium 82mg; Fibre 1.5g; Sodium 42mg.

Apple and cranberry muffins

Sweet and sharp and decidedly moreish, these muffins are richly spiced and packed with plenty of fruit flavour. Cranberries are considered a superfood with many health-boosting properties if eaten on a regular basis – a great ingredient to make a frequent feature of breakfast time.

4 In a large bowl, sift together the flour, baking powder, cinnamon, nutmeg, allspice, ginger and salt.

5 Make a well in the dry ingredients and pour in the egg mixture. With a spoon, stir until just blended.

6 Peel, core and quarter the apples. Chop the apple flesh coarsely with a sharp knife.

7 Add the apples, cranberries and walnuts to the batter and stir lightly to blend.

8 Three-quarters fill the cups. Bake for 25–30 minutes, until golden. Leave to stand for 5 minutes before transferring to a wire rack to go cold. Dust with icing sugar before serving. Store in an airtight container for up to 3 days.

MAKES 12 STANDARD MUFFINS

1 egg
50g/2oz/¼ cup butter, melted
100g/4oz/generous ½ cup caster
  (superfine) sugar
grated rind of 1 large orange
120ml/4fl oz/½ cup freshly
  squeezed orange juice
140g/5oz/1¼ cups plain
  (all-purpose) flour
5ml/1 tsp baking powder
2.5ml/½ tsp ground cinnamon
2.5ml/½ tsp freshly grated nutmeg
2.5ml/½ tsp ground allspice
pinch of ground ginger
2 small eating apples
170g/6oz/1½ cups cranberries
55g/2oz/1⅓ cups walnuts, chopped
icing (confectioners') sugar for
  dusting (optional)

1 Preheat the oven to 180°C/350°F/ Gas 4. Lightly grease the cups of a muffin tin (pan) or line them with paper cases.

2 In a bowl, whisk the egg with the melted butter to combine.

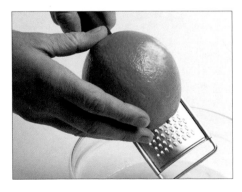

3 Add the sugar, grated orange rind and juice. Whisk to blend. Set aside.

Energy 149kcal/624kJ; Protein 2.5g; Carbohydrate 20.4g, of which sugars 10.8g; Fat 6.9g, of which saturates 2.6g; Cholesterol 25mg; Calcium 30mg; Fibre 0.9g; Sodium 34mg.

Pear and sultana bran muffins

These tasty muffins are best eaten freshly baked and served warm or cold, spread with butter, and a dollop of your favourite jam or honey. If you are counting the calories, eat them plain without any topping – they still taste good.

MAKES 12 STANDARD MUFFINS

75g/3oz/⅔ cup wholemeal
  (whole-wheat) flour
50g/2oz/½ cup plain
  (all-purpose) flour
50g/2oz/scant ½ cup bran
15ml/1 tbsp baking powder
50g/2oz/¼ cup butter, melted
50g/2oz/¼ cup soft light
  brown sugar
1 egg, beaten
200ml/7fl oz/scant 1 cup milk
50g/2oz/½ cup ready-to-eat dried
  pears, chopped
50g/2oz/⅓ cup sultanas
  (golden raisins)

1 Preheat the oven to 200°C/400°F/ Gas 6. Lightly grease the cups of a muffin tin (pan) or line them with paper cases.

2 Sift the flours, bran and baking powder into a large bowl.

3 In a jug (pitcher), mix together the melted butter, sugar, egg and milk and pour over the dry ingredients.

4 Gently fold the ingredients together. The mixture will be lumpy. Do not overmix.

5 Fold in the pears and sultanas.

6 Spoon the batter into the prepared paper cases. Bake for 15–20 minutes, until risen and golden.

7 Leave to stand for a few minutes, then turn out on to a wire rack to cool. Store in an airtight container for up to 3 days.

Energy 121kcal/510kJ; Protein 3g; Carbohydrate 18.7g, of which sugars 9.8g; Fat 4.3g, of which saturates 2.4g; Cholesterol 25mg; Calcium 51mg; Fibre 2.2g; Sodium 42mg.

Spiced sultana muffins

Weekend breakfasts will never be the same again once you have tried these delicious muffins! They are quick and easy to prepare and take only a short time to bake. The coconut milk adds enough sweetness to the recipe without the need for sugar.

MAKES 6 STANDARD MUFFINS

75g/3oz/6 tbsp butter, melted
1 small (US medium) egg
120ml/4fl oz/½ cup unsweetened coconut milk
150g/5oz/1¼ cups wholemeal (whole-wheat) flour
5ml/1 tsp baking powder
7.5ml/1½ tsp ground cinnamon
115g/4oz/⅔ cup sultanas (golden raisins)

1 Preheat the oven to 190°C/375°F/ Gas 5. Lightly grease the cups of a muffin tin (pan) or line them with paper cases.

2 Beat the butter, egg and coconut milk in a large bowl until blended.

VARIATION
Use currants or raisins, if you like.

3 Sift the flour, baking powder and cinnamon over the beaten mixture. Fold in gently.

4 Fold in the sultanas. Divide the batter among the muffin cups.

5 Bake for 20 minutes or until the muffins have risen well and are firm to the touch. Cool slightly on a wire rack before serving. Store in an airtight container for up to 3 days.

Energy 240kcal/1006kJ; Protein 4.9g; Carbohydrate 30.3g, of which sugars 14.9g; Fat 11.9g, of which saturates 6.9g; Cholesterol 58mg; Calcium 35mg; Fibre 2.6g; Sodium 114mg.

Apricot and orange buns

These moreish muffins are ideal as a late breakfast. They are finished with a slightly sour orange glaze that perfectly complements the sweetness of the cakes. If Seville oranges are not available, use a mixture of orange and lemon.

**MAKES 9–10 STANDARD
  MUFFINS**

1 egg, lightly beaten
175ml/6fl oz/¾ cup buttermilk
juice and rind of 1½ Seville
  (Temple) oranges
75g/3oz/6 tbsp butter, melted
225g/8oz/2 cups plain
  (all-purpose) flour
10ml/2 tsp baking powder
150g/5oz/¾ cup golden caster
  (superfine) sugar
15ml/1 tbsp Seville orange
  marmalade
115g/4oz dried apricots, chopped

For the orange glaze
juice and finely grated rind of
  ½ Seville (Temple) orange
75–90ml/5–6 tbsp icing
  (confectioners') sugar, sifted
5ml/1 tsp Seville orange
  marmalade

1 Preheat the oven to 180°C/350°F/ Gas 4. Line the cups of a muffin tin (pan) with paper cases.

2 In a bowl, mix together the egg, buttermilk, orange juice and grated rind and the cooled, melted butter.

3 Sift the flour with the baking powder into a large mixing bowl and stir in the sugar. Make a well in the centre of the dry ingredients.

4 Pour in the buttermilk mixture and fold it in gently, with the marmalade and the chopped apricots, until just blended. Do not overmix it.

5 Spoon the batter into the prepared paper cases, filling them almost to the top. Bake for 25 minutes until the cakes look golden and puffed up. Leave to stand in the tin for 5 minutes, then turn out on to a wire rack to go cold.

6 To make the orange glaze, put the juice in a bowl and slowly beat in the grated rind, icing sugar and marmalade. The mixture should cover the back of a spoon, but still be thin and fluid. Drizzle the glaze over the tops of the cakes about 10 minutes before serving, so it is fresh and shiny.

7 Serve immediately, or store without the glaze for up to 3 days.

Energy 211kcal/889kJ; Protein 3.5g; Carbohydrate 35.7g, of which sugars 18.6g; Fat 7g, of which saturates 4.3g; Cholesterol 37mg; Calcium 66mg; Fibre 0.7g; Sodium 75mg.

Fruity treats

Blueberries are one of the most popular additions to muffins, but whatever your favourite fruit, there is guaranteed to be a muffin recipe that incorporates it. Crunchy apples, sharp cranberries, sweet bananas, flavoursome peaches, dried cherries and exotic pineapple are all included in recipes in this lavish collection. Try blackberry and almond muffins with a hint of sloe gin and rose water, or apple and Calvados quince-glazed cakes for a mid-morning treat. Orange and poppy seed cakes drizzled with icing, or subtle apricot and maple syrup, make appealing alternatives. For a more substantial snack add an extra piece of fresh fruit and a dollop of yogurt or crème fraîche to the side.

Blackberry and almond muffins

Sloe gin and rose water add depth of flavour to these muffins, helping them to stand out from the crowd. Autumnal blackberries, picked in the countryside, are perfectly complemented by the mild flavour and crunch of blanched almonds. Store in an airtight container for up to three days.

MAKES 12 STANDARD MUFFINS

100g/3½oz/scant 1 cup fresh
  blackberries
300g/11oz/2¾ cups plain
  (all-purpose) flour
50g/2oz/¼ cup soft light
  brown sugar
20ml/4 tsp baking powder
60g/2¼oz/⅓ cup blanched
  almonds, chopped
2 eggs
100ml/3½fl oz/scant ½ cup milk
50g/2oz/¼ cup butter, melted
15ml/1 tbsp sloe gin
15ml/1 tbsp rose water

1 Preheat the oven to 200°C/400°F/ Gas 6. Line the cups of a muffin tin (pan) with paper cases.

2 Rinse the blackberries in a colander and pat dry.

3 Sift the flour, sugar and baking powder into a large bowl.

4 Stir in the almonds and black-berries, mixing them well to coat with the flour mixture. Make a well in the centre of the dry ingredients.

5 In another bowl, whisk the eggs wth the milk, then mix in the butter, sloe gin and rose water. Add to the dry ingredients and stir in.

6 Spoon the batter into the prepared paper cases and bake for 20–25 minutes or until golden. Leave to stand for 5 minutes before turning out on to a wire rack to go cool. Serve with butter, if you like.

Energy 181kcal/761kJ; Protein 4.8g; Carbohydrate 25g, of which sugars 5.8g; Fat 7.6g, of which saturates 2.9g; Cholesterol 42mg; Calcium 68mg; Fibre 1.4g; Sodium 49mg.

Dried cherry buns

Sold as a ready-to-eat snack food, dried cherries have a naturally tart flavour. They are a different product to glacé cherries, which are smothered in syrup. These scrumptious muffins taste delicious freshly baked and spread with butter and cherry jam.

MAKES 16 STANDARD MUFFINS

250ml/8fl oz/1 cup natural
   (plain) yogurt
225g/8oz/1 cup dried cherries
115g/4oz/¹/₂ cup butter, softened
175g/6oz/scant 1 cup caster
   (superfine) sugar
2 eggs
5ml/1 tsp vanilla extract
200g/7oz/1³/₄ cups plain
   (all-purpose) flour
10ml/2 tsp baking powder
5ml/1 tsp bicarbonate of soda
   (baking soda)

1 In a large bowl, combine the yogurt and dried cherries. Cover with clear film (plastic wrap) and leave to stand for about 30 minutes until the cherries plump up.

2 Preheat the oven to 180°C/350°F/ Gas 4. Lightly grease the cups of a muffin tin (pan) or line them with paper cases.

3 Beat together the butter and caster sugar in a bowl until it is light and fluffy. Add the eggs, one at a time, beating well after each addition until fully incorporated.

4 Add the vanilla extract and yogurt and cherry mixture. Stir until thoroughly combined.

5 Sift the flour, baking powder and bicarbonate of soda over the batter in batches. Gently fold in using a metal spoon.

6 Spoon the mixture into the paper cases, filling them two-thirds full. Bake for 20 minutes, or until risen and golden. Leave to stand in the tin for 5 minutes, then transfer to a wire rack to go completely cold. Eat fresh or store in an airtight container for up to 3 days.

Energy 187kcal/787kJ; Protein 3.1g; Carbohydrate 29.9g, of which sugars 20.4g; Fat 7g, of which saturates 4g; Cholesterol 39mg; Calcium 63mg; Fibre 0.6g; Sodium 73mg.

Cranberry and orange muffins

These delicious muffins are perfect to eat at any time of day and are a real energy boost for a mid-morning break or as a lunchbox treat. Use fresh or frozen cranberries; both will work well with this recipe. The orange zest adds to the tangy flavour of the cranberries.

4 Pour the egg mixture into the dry ingredients. Stir with a wooden spoon until just blended to a smooth batter.

5 Gently fold in the orange rind and cranberries with a metal spoon.

MAKES 10 STANDARD MUFFINS

350g/12oz/3 cups plain
 (all-purpose) flour, sifted
15ml/1 tsp baking powder
pinch of salt
115g/4oz/¹/₂ cup caster
 (superfine) sugar
2 eggs
150ml/¹/₄ pint/²/₃ cup milk
50ml/2fl oz/¹/₄ cup corn oil
finely grated rind of 1 orange
150g/5oz/1¹/₄ cups cranberries,
 thawed if frozen

1 Preheat the oven to 190°C/375°F/ Gas 5. Lightly grease the cups of a muffin tin (pan) or line them with paper cases.

2 Sift together the flour, baking powder and salt into a large bowl. Add the sugar and stir to mix. Make a well in the centre.

3 Using a fork, lightly beat the eggs with the milk and corn oil in another bowl, until they are thoroughly combined.

6 Fill the paper cases and bake for about 25 minutes, until risen and golden. Leave to stand for 5 minutes before transferring to a wire rack. Serve warm or cold. Store in an airtight container for up to 3 days.

COOK'S TIP
The tart flavour of cranberries is not to everyone's taste, but for those who enjoy a less sweet treat, these muffins are ideal.

Energy 221kcal/936kJ; Protein 5.1g; Carbohydrate 41.3g, of which sugars 14.6g; Fat 5.1g, of which saturates 1g; Cholesterol 39mg; Calcium 79mg; Fibre 1.3g; Sodium 24mg.

Apple and Calvados muffins with quince

A simple apple muffin is transformed into something much grander with the addition of luxurious French apple brandy and the aromatic flavour of quince. Quince glaze adds an appetizing shine to these wonderful autumnal muffins. Store in an airtight container for up to three days.

MAKES 10 STANDARD MUFFINS

250g/9oz/1¼ cups peeled and
    cored cooking apple flesh
30–45ml/2–3 tbsp quince paste
75g/3oz/6 tbsp butter
15ml/1 tbsp Calvados
225g/8oz/2 cups plain
    (all-purpose) flour
12.5ml/2½ tsp baking powder
85g/3oz/scant ⅓ cup caster
    (superfine) sugar
1 egg, lightly beaten
60ml/4 tbsp buttermilk
grated rind of 1 lemon

For the quince glaze
45ml/3 tbsp quince paste
5ml/1 tsp lemon juice
30ml/2 tbsp Calvados

1 Preheat the oven to 180°C /350°F/ Gas 4. Line the cups of a muffin tin (pan) with paper cases.

2 Chop most of the apples into cubes, and set aside. Cut a few into crescents and put in lemon water.

3 Put the quince paste and butter in a pan and stir until melted. Remove from the heat. Add the Calvados

4 Sift the flour, baking powder and sugar into a large bowl and form a well in the centre. Blend the egg and buttermilk. Pour into the dry ingredients with the lemon rind, Calvados mixture and apple. Stir until just blended.

5 Spoon the batter into the paper cases. Drain and slice the reserved apple segments into thin pieces and lightly press several on each muffin.

6 Bake for 25–30 minutes until golden and springy to the touch. Leave to stand for a few minutes then transfer to a wire rack.

7 To make the quince glaze, add the quince paste, lemon juice and 15ml/ 1 tbsp water to a small pan. Boil rapidly to make a thin syrup. Stir in the Calvados and simmer for 1 minute. Brush thickly over the surface of the warm muffins.

Energy 213kcal/899kJ; Protein 3.1g; Carbohydrate 34.1g, of which sugars 16.9g; Fat 7.1g, of which saturates 4.3g; Cholesterol 37mg; Calcium 50mg; Fibre 1.1g; Sodium 70mg.

Blueberry and cinnamon muffins

The traditional blueberry muffin is given a twist with the addition of warming cinnamon.
This sweet spice complements the fresh and juicy flavour of the berries. Eat while warm and fresh
from the oven, or enjoy them cold. Store in an airtight container for up to three days.

MAKES 8 STANDARD MUFFINS

115g/4oz/1 cup plain
  (all-purpose) flour
15ml/1 tbsp baking powder
pinch of salt
70g/2½oz/5 tbsp soft light
  brown sugar
10ml/2 tsp ground cinnamon
1 egg
175ml/6fl oz/¾ cup milk
45ml/3 tbsp vegetable oil
120g/4oz/1 cup blueberries

VARIATION
Peel and dice one apple and use
it in place of the blueberries.

1 Preheat the oven to 190°C/375°F/
Gas 5. Line the cups of a muffin tin
(pan) with paper cases.

2 Sift the flour, baking powder, salt
sugar and cinnamon into a bowl.
Add the egg, milk and vegetable oil
and whisk together until smooth.

3 Fold in the blueberries.

4 Spoon the batter into the muffin
cups, filling them two-thirds full.
Bake until a skewer inserted into the
centre of a muffin comes out clean,
about 25 minutes.

5 Leave to cool in the tin for
10 minutes, then turn out on to a
wire rack to go completely cold.

COOK'S TIP
Fresh blueberries are available
year round in supermarkets, but
they are naturally in season in
late summer, so this is the best
time to buy them – they are
likely to be sweeter and have a
better flavour.

Energy 141kcal/593kJ; Protein 3.1g; Carbohydrate 21.4g, of which sugars 10.5g; Fat 5.4g, of which saturates 0.9g; Cholesterol 25mg; Calcium 60mg; Fibre 0.9g; Sodium 19mg.

Raspberry muffins

Wholemeal flour makes these muffins a filling treat to keep hunger pangs at bay and with so little added sugar, they are healthier than most cakes. Raspberries are slightly acidic and bursting with goodness and flavour, and you can use frozen berries to make this recipe.

MAKES 10–12 STANDARD MUFFINS

120g/4oz/1 cup self-raising (self-rising) flour
120g/4oz/1 cup self-raising wholemeal (self-rising whole-wheat) flour
45ml/3 tbsp caster (superfine) sugar
2 eggs, beaten
200ml/7fl oz/scant 1 cup milk
50g/2oz/¼ cup butter, melted
175g/6oz/1½ cups raspberries, fresh or frozen (defrosted for less than 30 minutes)

1 Preheat the oven to 190°C/375°F/ Gas 5. Lightly grease the cups of a muffin tin (pan) or line them with paper cases.

2 Sift the dry ingredients together, then turn in the wholemeal flakes from the sieve (strainer). Make a well in the centre.

3 Beat the eggs, milk and melted butter together in a small bowl until thoroughly combined, then pour into the dry ingredients and mix to a smooth batter.

4 Add the raspberries and gently stir them in. (If you are using frozen raspberries, work quickly so that the cold berries remain solid.) If you mix too much, the raspberries will disintegrate.

5 Spoon the batter into the prepared paper cases. Bake for 30 minutes, until well risen and just firm. Leave to stand, then turn out on to a wire rack. Serve warm or cold. Store in an airtight container for up to 3 days.

Energy 132kcal/555kJ; Protein 4g; Carbohydrate 19g, of which sugars 5.7g; Fat 5g, of which saturates 2.7g; Cholesterol 42mg; Calcium 48mg; Fibre 1.5g; Sodium 45mg.

Orange poppy seed muffins

These muffins look attractive baked in large muffin cups and without paper cases so that the poppy-seed flecked sides of the cakes are visible. To serve, break open the freshly baked muffin and spread with butter and marmalade. Store without icing in an airtight container for three days.

4 Pour over the dry ingredients. Fold in until just mixed. Leave for 1 hour.

5 Preheat the oven to 180°C/350°F/ Gas 4.

MAKES 8 LARGE MUFFINS

275g/10oz/2½ cups plain
　(all-purpose) flour
150g/5oz/¾ cup caster
　(superfine) sugar
15ml/1 tbsp baking powder
2 eggs
75g/3oz/6 tbsp butter, melted
75ml/5 tbsp vegetable oil
20–25ml/1½tbsp poppy seeds
30ml/2tbsp orange juice, plus
　grated rind of 1½ oranges
5ml/1 tsp lemon juice, plus grated
　rind of 1 lemon

For the icing
25g/1oz/¼ cup icing
　(confectioners') sugar
15ml/1 tbsp orange juice

1 Lightly grease the cups of a muffin tin (pan) with melted butter or line them with paper cases.

2 Set aside 40g/1½oz of flour. Place the remaining flour with the dry ingredients in a mixing bowl. Make a well in the centre.

3 Mix the eggs, butter, oil, poppy seeds, citrus juices and rinds.

6 Fold the reserved flour into the batter but leave it lumpy.

7 Fill the muffin cups three-quarters full. Bake for 25 minutes, until risen and golden.

8 Leave to stand in the tin for a few minutes, then turn out on to a wire rack to go cold.

9 To make the icing, mix the icing sugar and orange juice in a bowl. Add a small quantity of water, if needed, to make a runny consistency. Drizzle over the cakes.

Energy 377kcal/1583kJ; Protein 5.7g; Carbohydrate 50.7g, of which sugars 24.5g; Fat 18.3g, of which saturates 7.5g; Cholesterol 89mg; Calcium 85mg; Fibre 1.2g; Sodium 107mg.

Apple and sour cream crumble muffins

Two-thirds of the cooking apples in this recipe are chopped and baked in the muffin batter. The remaining apples are sliced and coated in a sweet almond crumble, which makes a delicious crunchy texture for the muffin top. Store in an airtight container for up to three days.

MAKES 8 STANDARD MUFFINS

3 small cooking apples, peeled and cored
115g/4oz/½ cup caster (superfine) sugar, plus 10ml/2 tsp for coating
5ml/1 tsp ground cinnamon
250g/9oz/2¼ cups plain (all-purpose) flour
15ml/1 tbsp baking powder
75g/3oz/6 tbsp butter, melted
2 eggs, beaten
30ml/2 tbsp sour cream

For the cinnamon crumble
30ml/2 tbsp plain (all-purpose) flour
45ml/3 tbsp demerara (raw) sugar
30ml/2 tbsp ground almonds
pinch of ground cinnamon

1 Preheat the oven to 190°C/375°F/ Gas 5. Line the cups of a muffin tin (pan) with paper cases.

2 To make the crumble, mix all the ingredients together in a bowl. Cut one apple into thin crescents, and toss in the crumble. Set aside.

3 Dice the remaining apples. Sift 10ml/2 tsp sugar and the cinnamon over the top. Set aside.

4 Sift the flour, baking powder and sugar into a bowl. Stir in the melted butter, eggs and sour cream.

5 Add the apple chunks and lightly fold them into the batter.

6 Fill the paper cases with the batter, then arrange the crumble-coated apple on top.

7 Bake for 25 minutes until risen and golden. Cool on a wire rack.

Energy 272kcal/1144kJ; Protein 4.8g; Carbohydrate 42.8g, of which sugars 19g; Fat 10.2g, of which saturates 6g; Cholesterol 71mg; Calcium 65mg; Fibre 1.6g; Sodium 92mg.

Apricot and maple syrup muffins

Spelt flour has a nutty flavour and is slightly sweet. If you have trouble locating it, substitute plain wholegrain flour instead. Healthy and low in fat, serve these tall apricot muffins for afternoon tea – they're quite filling.

MAKES 8 TALL MUFFINS

175g/6oz/⅔ cup dried apricots
40g/1½oz/3 tbsp caster
  (superfine) sugar
150g/5oz/1¼ cups plain
  (all-purpose) flour
75g/3oz/⅔ cup spelt flour
10ml/2 tsp baking powder
2.5ml/½ tsp bicarbonate of soda
  (baking soda)
120ml/4fl oz/½ cup low-fat natural
  (plain) yogurt
1 egg, lightly beaten
60ml/4 tbsp maple syrup

1 Preheat the oven to 180°C/350°F/ Gas 4. Grease and line the dariole moulds with baking parchment.

2 Put the apricots in a pan with 30ml/2 tbsp water and the sugar. Bring slowly to the boil, stirring, then cover and leave to simmer for 4 minutes.

3 Mix the flours, baking powder and bicarbonate of soda in a large bowl and set aside.

4 Drain the apricots, reserving the syrup. Cut the apricots into quarters.

5 In a small bowl, mix the yogurt, egg, maple syrup and reserved syrup and pour them over the dry ingredients. Fold lightly in with the chopped apricot until just combined.

6 Spoon into the lined moulds and bake for 18 minutes. Leave to stand then transfer to a wire rack to cool completely. Store in an airtight container for up to 3 days.

COOK'S TIP
If you don't have dariole moulds, use a standard muffin tin (pan) lined with paper cases and bake for 22–24 minutes.

Energy 187kcal/796kJ; Protein 5.4g; Carbohydrate 40.8g, of which sugars 20.7g; Fat 1.4g, of which saturates 0.3g; Cholesterol 24mg; Calcium 83mg; Fibre 2.8g; Sodium 46mg.

Blueberry and vanilla muffins

Vanilla extract has a sweet aroma and intense, easily identifiable flavour. In this recipe it is used to enhance the natural taste of the juicy blueberries. These muffins are perfect for a mid-afternoon treat to keep hunger pangs at bay. Store in an airtight container for up to three days.

MAKES 12 STANDARD MUFFINS

350g/12oz/3 cups plain
  (all-purpose) flour
10ml/2 tsp baking powder
115g/4oz/½ cup caster
  (superfine) sugar
2 eggs, beaten
300ml/½ pint/1¼ cups milk
120g/4oz/½ cup butter, melted
5ml/1 tsp vanilla extract
170g/6oz/1½ cups blueberries

1 Preheat the oven to 200°C/400°F/
Gas 6. Line the cups of a muffin tin
(pan) with paper cases.

2 Sift the flour and baking powder
into a bowl. Stir in the sugar.

3 In another bowl, whisk together
the eggs, milk, butter and vanilla.

4 Fold the egg mixture into the dry
ingredients with a metal spoon, then
gently stir in the blueberries.

5 Spoon the batter into the prepared
paper cases, filling them until just
below the top. Fill any empty cups
half full with water to prevent
burning. Bake for 20–25 minutes,
until the muffins are well risen and
lightly browned.

6 Leave the muffins in the tin for
5 minutes and then turn them out
on to a wire rack to cool. Serve
warm or cold with a spoonful of
berry preserve.

Energy 243kcal/1021kJ; Protein 4.9g; Carbohydrate 35.9g, of which sugars 13.1g; Fat 9.9g, of which saturates 6g; Cholesterol 56mg; Calcium 82mg; Fibre 1.2g; Sodium 102mg.

Banana and pecan muffins

The rich, buttery flavour of pecan nuts complements the sweetness of banana in these deliciously moreish muffins. Pecans are a healthy treat, and can be stored in the freezer for convenience. Serve these muffins warm and freshly baked, or store in an airtight container for up to three days.

3 In a large bowl, beat together the butter and sugar until light and fluffy.

4 Add the egg and vanilla and beat until smooth. Mix in the bananas.

5 With the mixer on low speed, beat in the flour mixture, alternating it with the milk. Add the pecans.

MAKES 8 STANDARD MUFFINS

150g/5oz/1¼ cups plain
   (all-purpose) flour
7.5ml/1½ tsp baking powder
55g/2oz/¼ cup butter, softened
150g/5oz/¾ cup caster
   (superfine) sugar
1 egg
5ml/1 tsp vanilla extract
3 bananas, mashed
75ml/5 tbsp milk
55g/2oz/⅓ cup pecans, chopped,
   plus extra for decorating
   (optional)

1 Preheat the oven to 190°C/375°F/ Gas 5. Line the cups of a muffin tin (pan) with paper cases.

2 Sift the flour and baking powder into a small bowl. Set aside.

6 Spoon the batter into the paper cases, filling them two-thirds full. Bake until golden brown and a skewer inserted into the centre comes out clean, 20–25 minutes. Decorate with extra pecans.

7 Leave to cool in the tin for 10 minutes, then transfer to a wire rack. Let cool 10 minutes longer before serving.

Energy 277kcal/1164kJ; Protein 4g; Carbohydrate 43.7g, of which sugars 28.5g; Fat 10.7g, of which saturates 4g; Cholesterol 38mg; Calcium 58mg; Fibre 1.3g; Sodium 53mg.

Coconut and rum muffins

Malibu is an intoxicating mix of pineapple juice, coconut milk and white rum. If it's your favourite tipple, then you'll love these muffins, because the same indulgent ingredient combination is used. Make these for a special occasion. Store in an airtight container for up to three days.

MAKES 8 STANDARD MUFFINS

175g/6oz fresh pineapple, plus
   extra for decoration
115g/4oz/½ cup natural glacé
   (candied) cherries, halved, plus
   extra for decoration
45ml/3 tbsp white rum
225g/8oz/2 cups plain
   (all-purpose) flour
10ml/2 tsp baking powder
175g/6oz/¾ cup butter, softened
175g/6oz/¾ cup soft light
   brown sugar
2 eggs
7.5ml/1½tsp vanilla extract
75ml/2½fl oz/⅓ cup coconut milk
icing (confectioners') sugar,
   for dusting

1 Cut the pineapple into segments, then into thin slices. Put in a small bowl with the glacé cherries. Pour over the rum and leave to marinate for 30–60 minutes.

2 Preheat the oven to 180°C/350°F/ Gas 4. Line the cups of a muffin tin (pan) with paper cases.

3 Sift the flour and the baking powder into a large bowl. Set aside.

4 In a bowl, beat the butter and sugar until light and creamy, then gradually beat in the eggs, one at a time. Stir in the vanilla and coconut milk and mix well.

5 Add the rum-soaked fruit in small amounts with the flour and baking powder mixture until just combined.

6 Divide the batter between the paper cases and decorate the tops with extra thin pieces of pineapple and cherry halves.

7 Bake for 20–25 minutes until golden on top and springy to touch.

8 Leave to cool slightly then turn out on to a wire rack to go cold. Serve warm.

Energy 420kcal/1764kJ; Protein 4.6g; Carbohydrate 56.9g, of which sugars 35.4g; Fat 19.7g, of which saturates 12.3g; Cholesterol 98mg; Calcium 76mg; Fibre 1.3g; Sodium 197mg.

Lemon and elderflower poppy seed muffins

Poppy seeds add an unexpectedly light and crunchy texture to the cake crumb, which traditionally is soaked in a sweet lemon syrup. For a breakfast treat, omit the syrup, break open the freshly baked muffin and spread it with butter and fresh lemon curd instead.

4 Pour the liquid into the flour mix and stir until just combined.

5 Fill the lined moulds three-quarters full and bake for 25 minutes. Leave to stand for a few minutes, then transfer to a wire rack to go cold.

MAKES 8 TALL MUFFINS

225g/8oz/2 cups self-raising (self-rising) flour
200g/7oz/1 cup caster (superfine) sugar
40g/1½oz ground almonds
2 eggs, beaten
75g/3oz/6 tbsp butter, melted
50ml/2fl oz/¼ cup vegetable oil
25ml/1½ tbsp poppy seeds
30ml/2 tbsp lemon juice
grated rind of 1 lemon
grated rind of 1 clementine

For the syrup
115g/4oz/generous ½ cup caster (superfine) sugar
50ml/2fl oz /¼ cup lemon juice
15ml/1 tbsp elderflower cordial
lemon segments, to decorate

1 Preheat the oven to 180°C/350°F/ Gas 4. Grease and line 8 dariole moulds with baking parchment.

2 Sift the flour and sugar into a bowl. Stir in the ground almonds. Make a well in the centre.

3 In a jug (pitcher) mix together the eggs, butter, oil, poppy seeds, lemon juice and the grated fruit rinds.

6 To make the syrup, put the sugar, 120ml/4fl oz/½ cup water and the lemon juice in a pan and heat gently, stirring frequently until dissolved.

7 Leave to boil without stirring for 5–6 minutes until syrupy. Remove from the heat. Stir in the cordial.

8 Prick holes in the top of each muffin using a skewer. Pour over the warm syrup. Store for up to 1 week. Decorate the muffin tops with thin segments of lemon, before serving.

Energy 408kcal/1717kJ; Protein 5.9g; Carbohydrate 63.9g, of which sugars 42.4g; Fat 16.1g, of which saturates 6.2g; Cholesterol 69mg; Calcium 94mg; Fibre 1.4g; Sodium 92mg.

Peach and almond muffins

Ripe peaches with their soft, juicy flesh, velvety coat and distinctive scent are synonymous with late summer. These luxurious fruits make a delightful addition to muffins. Use them when they are in season and fully mature for the best flavour. Use nectarines, if you prefer. Eat fresh.

MAKES 8 STANDARD MUFFINS

2 large ripe peaches
225g/8oz/2 cups plain
   (all-purpose) flour
15ml/1 tbsp baking powder
150g/5oz/¾ cup caster
   (superfine) sugar
40g/1½oz ground almonds
2 eggs
75g/3oz/6 tbsp butter, melted
50ml/2fl oz/¼ cup sunflower oil
20ml/4 tsp sour cream
15ml/1 tbsp flaked (sliced)
   almonds, for sprinkling
icing (confectioners') sugar,
   for dusting
passion fruit and lime curd (see
   page 16), to serve

1 Preheat the oven to 180°C/350°F/ Gas 4. Line the cups of a muffin tin (pan) with paper cases.

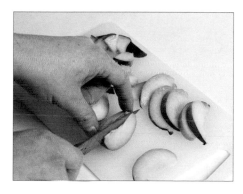

2 Cut one peach into small chunks to add to the batter. Cut the other peach into thin crescents and set aside for the topping.

3 Sift the flour, baking powder and sugar into a bowl. Stir in the ground almonds. Form a well in the centre.

4 In a jug (pitcher), whisk together the eggs, melted butter, oil and sour cream until combined. Pour into the dry ingredients and partly fold in. Add the chopped peaches and fold in until just combined.

5 Divide the batter between the paper cases.

6 Decorate the top of each with sliced fruit crescents. Sprinkle over the flaked almonds.

7 Bake for 28 minutes. Leave to stand in the tin for a few minutes, then transfer to a wire rack to cool. Dust with icing sugar and serve with passion fruit and lime curd.

Energy 326kcal/1369kJ; Protein 5.7g; Carbohydrate 43.8g, of which sugars 22.2g; Fat 15.5g, of which saturates 6.4g; Cholesterol 71mg; Calcium 74mg; Fibre 1.6g; Sodium 92mg.

Sweet vegetable and herb muffins

We think of vegetables and herbs as the mainstay of savoury dishes, but many hold their own in desserts, tarts and cakes. Pumpkins, carrots, sweet potatoes, courgettes and even beetroot all make fine additions to sweet muffins. Herbs feature too, imparting familiar and delicate scents. Muffins made with vegetables have a moist texture, which in turn gives them a longer shelf life. Try caramelized pear with cumin and rosemary, marigold flower corn muffins, or rich and flavoursome beetroot and dark chocolate muffins.

Pumpkin muffins

Small pumpkin varieties produce muffins with the sweetest taste. Select a pumpkin that is heavy for its size because it will have more moisture and be less likely to be stringy in texture. Nutmeg and currants make the perfect flavour partners for pumpkin. Keep for up to one week.

MAKES 14 STANDARD MUFFINS

115g/4oz/½ cup butter, softened
150g/5oz/¾ cup soft dark brown
  sugar
60ml/4 tbsp molasses
225g/8oz cooked pumpkin
1 egg, beaten
225g/8oz/2 cups plain
  (all-purpose) flour
5ml/1 tsp bicarbonate of soda
  (baking soda)
7.5ml/1½ tsp ground cinnamon
5ml/1 tsp freshly grated nutmeg
25g/1oz/2 tbsp currants or raisins

1 Preheat the oven to 200°C/400°F/ Gas 6. Line the cups of a muffin tin (pan) with paper cases.

2 In a large bowl, beat the butter and sugar until light and fluffy. Beat in the molasses.

3 Mash the pumpkin so that it is almost smooth (some lumps add to the texture), then add it with the egg to the butter and sugar mixture and stir until well blended.

4 Sift over the flour, bicarbonate of soda, cinnamon and nutmeg. Fold just enough to blend.

5 Fold in the currants or raisins. Spoon the batter into paper cases, filling them three-quarters full.

6 Bake until the tops spring back when touched lightly, 12–15 minutes. Leave to stand for 5 minutes, before transferring to a wire rack to cool.

COOK'S TIP
To cook the pumpkin, cut into segments, remove the seeds and pith, place in a baking tray with 6mm/¼in water and bake for 1 hour at 150°C/300°F/Gas 3. Remove the skin and mash.

Energy 216kcal/906kJ; Protein 2.2g; Carbohydrate 32.5g, of which sugars 21.5g; Fat 9.4g, of which saturates 5.7g; Cholesterol 36mg; Calcium 84mg; Fibre 0.7g; Sodium 86mg.

Carrot muffins

Sweet and moist and subtly flavoured with cinnamon and nutmeg, these bitesize carrot muffins are perfect for a lunchbox treat. They're also deliciously moreish, and one just might not be enough, so make plenty to share with friends. Keep for up to one week.

MAKES 12 STANDARD MUFFINS

175g/6oz/³/₄ cup butter, softened
90g/3¹/₂oz/scant ¹/₂ cup soft dark
   brown sugar
1 egg
225g/8oz/1³/₄ cups carrots, grated
140g/5oz/1¹/₄ cups plain
   (all-purpose) flour
5ml/1 tsp baking powder
2.5ml/¹/₂ tsp bicarbonate of soda
   (baking soda)
5ml/1 tsp ground cinnamon
pinch of freshly grated nutmeg

1 Preheat the oven to 180°C/350°F/ Gas 4. Lightly grease the cups of a muffin tin (pan).

2 Cream the butter and sugar until light and fluffy. Beat in the egg and 15ml/1 tbsp water.

3 Stir in the carrots.

4 Sift over the flour, baking powder, bicarbonate of soda, cinnamon and nutmeg. Stir to blend.

5 Spoon the batter into the prepared tin, filling the cups almost full.

6 Bake until the tops spring back when touched lightly, about 35 minutes. Let stand for 10 minutes before transferring to a wire rack.

Energy 248kcal/1035kJ; Protein 3.6g; Carbohydrate 21.5g, of which sugars 15g; Fat 17g, of which saturates 4.4g; Cholesterol 36mg; Calcium 35mg; Fibre 1.6g; Sodium 47mg.

Sweet potato and raisin muffins

An unusual ingredient in cakes, sweet potatoes are a great vegetable to bake with. Their natural sweet flavour and bright orange colouring is enhanced by the addition of raisins to produce a batter that bakes into a light but moist muffin. Store in an airtight container for three days.

MAKES 12 STANDARD MUFFINS

225g/8oz sweet potato
350g/12oz/3 cups plain
 (all-purpose) flour
15ml/1 tbsp baking powder
1 egg, beaten
225g/8oz/1 cup butter, melted
250ml/8fl oz/1 cup milk
50g/2oz/scant ½ cup raisins
50g/2oz/¼ cup caster (superfine)
 sugar
icing (confectioners') sugar,
 for dusting

1 Cut the sweet potato into chunks and cook in boiling water for 45 minutes, or until very tender. Drain the potato and when cool enough to handle, peel off the skin. Place in a large bowl and mash well.

2 Preheat the oven to 220°C/425°F/ Gas 7. Lightly grease the cups of a muffin tin (pan) or line them with paper cases.

3 Sift the flour and baking powder over the potato. Stir in, then beat in the egg. Whisk the butter and milk together then add to the batter.

4 Add the raisins and sugar and mix the ingredients together.

5 Spoon the batter into the prepared paper cases, filling them almost to the top.

6 Bake for 25 minutes until golden. Leave to stand in the tin for 5 minutes before turning out on to a wire rack to cool. Dust with icing sugar and serve warm.

Energy 297kcal/1245kJ; Protein 4.4g; Carbohydrate 34.9g, of which sugars 9.8g; Fat 16.6g, of which saturates 10.5g; Cholesterol 60mg; Calcium 80mg; Fibre 1.4g; Sodium 169mg.

Beetroot and bitter chocolate muffins

Although it is not often used in baking, freshly cooked beetroot contrasts well with the intense cocoa flavour of bitter chocolate. Because the muffins are coated with chocolate frosting they should be consumed quickly, or kept refrigerated for no more than two days.

**MAKES 9–10 STANDARD
    MUFFINS**

115g/4oz dark (bittersweet)
    chocolate
115g/4oz/½ cup butter
250g/9oz beetroot (beets), cooked
    and peeled
3 eggs, lightly beaten
225g/8oz/2 cups self-raising
    (self-rising) flour
2.5ml/½ tsp baking powder
200g/7oz/1 cup caster
    (superfine) sugar
20–30ml/1½–2 tbsp rye flour,
    for dusting
chocolate frosting, for topping
    (see page 76)

1 Preheat the oven to 180°C/350°F/ Gas 4. Lightly grease the cups of a muffin tin (pan) or line them with paper cases.

2 Melt the chocolate and butter in a large heatproof bowl set over a pan of barely simmering water. Stir occasionally. Remove from the heat.

3 Grate the cooked beetroot using the medium blade of a cheese grater.

4 Whisk the beetroot into the chocolate and butter mixture with the eggs.

5 Sift the flour, baking powder and sugar into the mixture and fold in gently. Do not overmix. Spoon the batter into the prepared tin. Dust with the rye flour.

6 Bake for 25 minutes until risen and springy to the touch. Leave to cool for 5 minutes, then transfer to a wire rack to go completely cold.

7 Spread the tops with chocolate frosting. Eat fresh for best taste.

COOK'S TIP
To cook beetroot, trim the stems 2.5cm/1in above the bulbs, taking care not to tear the skin. Place the beetroot in a pan of boiling water and boil for 1½ hours until tender. Drain, and when cool, nip off the stems and roots. Peel away the skin.

Energy 342kcal/1437kJ; Protein 5.4g; Carbohydrate 50g, of which sugars 30.2g; Fat 14.8g, of which saturates 8.7g; Cholesterol 85mg; Calcium 112mg; Fibre 1.5g; Sodium 218mg.

Sweet marrow muffins

Marrow, flaked almonds, golden syrup and vanilla make an unusual muffin with a delicate flavour. These muffins will remain moist for up to one week, if they are kept in an airtight container, and will also freeze well for a future occasion.

MAKES 10 STANDARD MUFFINS

300g/11oz marrow (large zucchini)
100ml/3½fl oz/½ cup olive oil
225g/8oz/generous 1 cup soft light
  brown sugar
2 small (US medium) eggs
7.5ml/1½ tsp vanilla extract
30ml/2 tbsp golden (light
  corn) syrup
175g/6oz/generous 1 cup sultanas
  (golden raisins)
50g/2oz/½ cup flaked (sliced)
  almonds
250g/9oz/2¼ cups self-raising
  (self-rising) flour
pinch of salt
7.5ml/1½ tsp mixed (pumpkin
  pie) spice

1 Preheat the oven to 180°C/350°F/ Gas 4. Lightly grease the cups of a muffin tin (pan) or line them with paper cases.

2 To prepare the marrow, peel and remove the central core of seeds. Grate the flesh. Set aside on kitchen paper to drain.

3 In a bowl, beat the oil with the sugar, then add the eggs, one at a time, beating until the mixture forms a pale batter. Add the vanilla and golden syrup and stir well to combine.

4 Add the grated marrow flesh and the sultanas, then stir in the flaked almonds.

5 Sift the flour, salt and spice together and fold the mixture lightly into the cake batter. Do not overmix. Divide the batter between the prepared paper cases.

6 Bake for 25–30 minutes, until risen and golden. Leave to stand for a few minutes before turning out on to a wire rack to cool completely. Serve with tea.

Energy 338kcal/1427kJ; Protein 5.7g; Carbohydrate 57.8g, of which sugars 39.1g; Fat 11g, of which saturates 1.6g; Cholesterol 38mg; Calcium 137mg; Fibre 1.8g; Sodium 118mg.

Caramelized pear and herb muffins

Many muffins make excellent desserts and this is certainly one of them. Serve hot with crème fraîche or fresh vanilla custard. Spoonfuls of warm caramel sauce to drizzle on top adds a touch of luxury. The sweetness is offset by the addition of aromatic rosemary and cumin. Eat fresh.

MAKES 6 LARGE MUFFINS

3 ripe pears, peeled
40g/1½oz unsalted butter, for frying the pears
15ml/1 tbsp caster (superfine) sugar, for frying the pears
2 eggs
200ml/7fl oz/scant 1 cup buttermilk
5ml/1 tsp fresh rosemary, finely chopped, plus extra to decorate
75g/3oz/6 tbsp butter, melted
225g/8oz/2 cups plain (all-purpose) flour
10ml/2 tsp baking powder
150g/5oz/generous ½ cup caster (superfine) sugar
60ml/4 tbsp warm caramel sauce (see page 18), to serve
5ml/1 tsp cumin seeds

1 Preheat the oven to 190°C/375°F/Gas 5. Lightly grease 6 large cups of a muffin tin (pan).

2 Cut the stalk end off the pears. Dice the flesh from the stalk end and set aside.

3 Cut the rest of the pears in half and remove the cores. Slice the flesh.

4 Melt the butter in a frying pan. Add the pear slices, sugar and 45–50ml/3–4 tbsp water. Fry gently for 6 minutes, or until the pears caramelize. Set aside.

5 In a bowl, beat the eggs with the buttermilk and chopped rosemary, then stir in the melted butter.

6 In a large bowl, sift together the flour, baking powder and sugar. Make a well in the centre.

7 Pour the liquid into the dry ingredients and partly blend. Add the chopped pears and continue to mix lightly until the batter is evenly blended. Do not overmix.

8 Spoon the batter into the prepared muffin tins, filling them half full. Add two caramelized pear segments to each. Add a teaspoon of caramel sauce and smooth it with a knife. Sprinkle over the cumin seeds.

9 Bake for 25–30 minutes, or until a skewer inserted in the centre of a muffin comes out clean, and the tops are springy to the touch.

10 Leave to cool slightly in the tin, then transfer to warmed plates. Decorate with fresh rosemary, drizzle with a little extra warmed caramel sauce and serve immediately.

Energy 486kcal/2045kJ; Protein 7.3g; Carbohydrate 74.1g, of which sugars 45.5g; Fat 20g, of which saturates 12.2g; Cholesterol 113mg; Calcium 133mg; Fibre 2.8g; Sodium 192mg.

Marigold flower corn muffins

These are moist and light corn muffins, which are best served cold, spread with butter and a generous spoonful of a scented apple, crab apple or quince jam. Make sure you use English marigolds (*Calendula*), not *Tagetes* varieties. Keep in an airtight container for three days.

5 Sift the flour and baking powder into the butter mixture and fold in. Stir in the ground almonds and cornmeal until just combined.

6 Add the orange juice, taking care not to overmix the ingredients.

7 Spoon the batter into the prepared dariole moulds. Sprinkle over the marigold flower petals.

8 Bake for 22–25 minutes, until well risen and golden. Leave to cool slightly, then transfer to a wire rack to go cold.

MAKES 5–6 TALL MUFFINS

50g/2oz/¼ cup butter, softened
90g/3½oz/½ cup caster (superfine) sugar
2 eggs
5ml/1 tsp finely grated lemon rind
40g/1½oz sour cream
150g/5oz/1¼ cups plain (all-purpose) flour
10ml/2 tsp baking powder
25g/1oz ground almonds
50g/2oz/½ cup cornmeal (polenta)
45ml/3 tbsp orange juice
20–25 marigold flower petals

1 Preheat the oven to 180°C/350°F/ Gas 4. Lightly grease 5–6 dariole moulds and line them with baking parchment.

2 In a large bowl, cream the butter and sugar until light and fluffy.

3 Beat in the eggs, one at a time, adding 15ml/1 tbsp sifted flour with each egg to prevent the mixture from curdling.

4 Stir in the lemon rind with the sour cream.

VARIATION
You could also use lavender florets in these muffins.

Energy 303kcal/1271kJ; Protein 6.5g; Carbohydrate 42.4g, of which sugars 17.1g; Fat 12.9g, of which saturates 6.1g; Cholesterol 87mg; Calcium 71mg; Fibre 1.3g; Sodium 92mg.

Courgette and raisin muffins

These muffins are delicious, so if you're a keen gardener with a glut of courgettes to use up, ring the changes by making a sweet treat. The muffins are baked in terracotta pots, which are available from good cookware shops. Keep for up to one week in an airtight container.

MAKES 10 LARGE MUFFINS

150g/5oz courgettes (zucchini)
115g/4oz/1 cup pine nuts
200g/7oz/1 cup caster
   (superfine) sugar
2 eggs
115g/4oz/½ cup butter, melted
175g/6oz/1½ cup plain
   (all-purpose) flour
7.5ml/1½ tsp baking powder
115g/4oz/scant 1 cup raisins

1 Preheat the oven to 180°C/350°F/ Gas 4. Grease and line the terracotta pots with a square of baking parchment.

2 Cut each courgette into fine julienned strips, then place on to kitchen paper and set aside to drain.

3 Spread the pine nuts on to a baking sheet and bake for 1½–2 minutes until golden (watch carefully as they burn quickly).

4 In a large bowl, beat together the sugar and eggs for 1 minute. Add the melted butter and beat for another minute. Sift in the flour and baking powder. Fold in until partly blended.

5 Stir in the raisins, grated courgettes and the toasted pine nuts until evenly blended. Do not overmix.

6 Spoon the batter into the prepared terracotta pots and bake for 25–30 minutes until well risen and golden and the tops spring back when touched. Leave to stand for a few minutes, then turn out on to a wire rack to go cold or serve in the pots.

Energy 351kcal/1471kJ; Protein 5.2g; Carbohydrate 43.2g, of which sugars 29.8g; Fat 18.7g, of which saturates 7.1g; Cholesterol 65mg; Calcium 53mg; Fibre 1.1g; Sodium 109mg.

Cornmeal, orange and rosemary muffins

Cornmeal (sometimes called maize meal or polenta) provides these muffins with a glorious yellow crumb which is delicately flavoured with fresh rosemary. The sweet syrup adds an extra citrus hit as well as a glossy finish to the baked muffins. Keep for three days in an airtight container.

MAKES 10–11 STANDARD MUFFINS

2 oranges
4 eggs
115g/4oz/²⁄₃ cup cornmeal (polenta)
115g/4oz/1 cup ground almonds
225g/8oz/generous 1 cup caster (superfine) sugar
15ml/1 tbsp fresh rosemary, finely chopped
75g/3oz/³⁄₄ cup self-raising (self-rising) flour

For the syrup
50ml/2fl oz/¼ cup orange juice
50g/2oz/¼ cup caster (superfine) sugar
2.5ml/½ tsp fresh rosemary, finely chopped
rind of ¼ orange, cut into very thin 2cm/¾in long strips

1 Place the whole oranges in a pan of boiling water and leave to boil for 2 hours, until soft. Remove from the pan and leave to cool.

2 Preheat the oven to 180°C/350°F/ Gas 4. Line the cups of a muffin tin (pan) with paper cases.

3 Split the fruit. Remove the pips (seeds). Purée the orange and skin using a blender until smooth.

4 In a large bowl, whisk together the purée, eggs, polenta, ground almonds and sugar.

5 Add the rosemary. Sift over the flour and stir in until just blended.

6 Spoon the batter into the paper cases and bake for 25 minutes, or until light golden and springy to the touch. Leave in the tin to cool slightly, then turn out on to a wire rack.

7 To make the syrup, put 25ml/ 1½ tbsp water with the remaining ingredients in a small pan and bring slowly to the boil, stirring frequently. Boil for 3–4 minutes, then remove from the heat. Prick the surface of the warm muffins and pour over the warm syrup, until it is all used up.

Energy 259kcal/1089kJ; Protein 6.4g; Carbohydrate 41.6g, of which sugars 28.6g; Fat 8.3g, of which saturates 1.1g; Cholesterol 69mg; Calcium 82mg; Fibre 1.5g; Sodium 54mg.

Caraway seed muffins with lemon glaze

The tiny slender seed of the caraway plant has a distinctive aromatic scent and slightly hot flavour, which resembles aniseed when it is added to breads and cakes. Serve these muffins while they are warm. Spread with butter, or add the syrupy lemon glaze for a sweeter tea-time treat.

3 Beat in the eggs, then sift over half of the flour and baking powder. Stir lightly to combine.

4 In a small bowl, whisk together the milk, vanilla and caraway seeds.

5 Pour the liquid into the batter with the remaining flour. Mix lightly.

6 Divide the batter between the prepared cups and bake for 25 minutes, until springy to the touch. Leave to cool slightly, then transfer to a wire rack.

7 To make the topping, in a bowl, mix the glaze ingredients together with 15ml/1 tbsp boiling water until smooth and the consistency of thin cream. Drizzle over the tops of the warm cakes. Keep for up to 1 week.

MAKES 8 LARGE MUFFINS

175g/6oz/¾ cup butter, softened
175g/6oz/scant 1 cup caster (superfine) sugar
3 eggs, lightly beaten
225g/8oz/2 cups plain (all-purpose) flour
5ml/1 tsp baking powder
30ml/2 tbsp milk
5ml/1 tsp vanilla extract
15ml/1 tbsp caraway seeds

For the lemon glaze
75g/3oz/¾ cup icing (confectioners') sugar, sifted
10–15ml/2–3 tsp lemon juice

1 Preheat the oven to 180°C/350°F/ Gas 4. Lightly grease the cups of a muffin tin (pan) or line them with paper cases.

2 In a mixing bowl, beat the butter and sugar until light and fluffy.

Energy 410kcal/1718kJ; Protein 5.4g; Carbohydrate 54.7g, of which sugars 33.3g; Fat 20.4g, of which saturates 12.5g; Cholesterol 122mg; Calcium 74mg; Fibre 0.9g; Sodium 195mg.

Sweet and indulgent muffins

Sweet scrumptious muffins, packed with luxurious ingredients and iced with decadent frostings, are a pleasure intended for sharing. This chapter tempts the palate with an enticing collection of recipes featuring everyone's favourite ingredients. Try raspberry and white chocolate muffins filled with a mousse-like truffle, or rich and crunchy coffee and macadamia nut muffins. Banoffee muffins are topped with bananas and drizzled with caramel sauce and are perfect for every sweet tooth. There are ideas too for children's parties: Halloween muffins topped with spooky frosting and decorated with ghostly shapes, or cute chocolate muffins topped with confectionery.

Spice muffins with dove-shaped cookies

This muffin recipe has three personalities. Warm from the oven and spread with butter it makes a light breakfast treat; decorated with a cookie it makes a filling cake for tea time; add the simple frosting and you have a luxurious creation for a special occasion. Eat fresh.

MAKES 5 JUMBO MUFFINS

90g/3½oz/½ cup golden caster
   (superfine) sugar
200g/7oz/scant 1 cup clear honey
grated rind of 1 large orange
150g/5oz/1¼ cups rye flour
175g/6oz/1½ cups plain
   (all-purpose) flour
10ml/2 tsp baking powder
pinch of mixed (apple pie) spice
pinch of ground cloves
pinch of ground cinnamon
1 egg yolk

For the dove cookies
50g/2oz/¼ cup soft light brown
   sugar
50g/2oz/4 tbsp butter, softened
90g/3½oz/scant 1 cup plain
   (all-purpose) flour
5ml/1 tsp baking powder
2.5ml/½ tsp ground cinnamon
2.5ml/½ tsp ground ginger
2.5ml/½ tsp freshly grated nutmeg
12.5ml/2½ tsp milk, or buttermilk

For the frosting
1 egg white
icing (confectioners') sugar, sifted
silver balls for eyes

1 Preheat the oven to 180°C/350°F/ Gas 4. Line the cups of a jumbo muffin tin (pan) with paper cases.

2 To make the muffins, put 120ml/ 4fl oz/¼ cup water, the sugar, honey and orange rind in a small pan and heat gently until the sugar dissolves, stirring occasionally. Leave to cool slightly.

3 Sift the flours, baking powder and spices into a large bowl. Make a well in the centre.

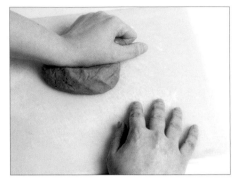

4 Add half the honey liquid with the egg yolk and stir lightly. Add the remaining honey liquid and stir until just combined.

5 Spoon the batter into the paper cases. Bake for 30–35 minutes until risen and golden, then leave to stand for a few minutes. Transfer to a wire rack to cool completely.

6 Turn the oven to 150°C/300°F/ Gas 2. Lightly grease a baking sheet.

7 To make the cookies, in a bowl, beat the sugar and butter together. Sift in the dry ingredients and mix to combine, adding milk as you work.

8 Knead the dough lightly with your hands until smooth.

9 On a lightly floured surface, roll the dough to a 5mm/¼in thickness and cut out doves.

10 Place on the baking sheet and bake for 17–18 minutes. Leave to set for a few minutes on the sheet, then carefully transfer to a wire rack to go completely cold.

11 Mix the frosting ingredients together and spread most over the tops of the muffins, reserving a little of the frosting to decorate the cookies.

12 Fill a piping bag fitted with a plain nozzle with the reserved frosting. Pipe your choice of decoration. Add an eye.

Energy 601kcal/2549kJ; Protein 8.8g; Carbohydrate 124.8g, of which sugars 60.6g; Fat 10.9g, of which saturates 6g; Cholesterol 63mg; Calcium 112mg; Fibre 5.2g; Sodium 86mg.

Chocolate and walnut muffins

This muffin offers the perfect combination for chocoholics – cocoa powder and added chocolate chunks. The dense and sweet chocolate batter is not for the faint-hearted. It's deliciously moist and moreish, and the chopped walnuts add crunch and texture. Will keep for up to one week.

MAKES 12 STANDARD MUFFINS

175g/6oz/¾ cup unsalted butter
140g/5oz/1¼ cups plain
   (semisweet) chocolate
200g/7oz/1 cup caster
   (superfine) sugar
55g/2oz/¼ cup soft dark
   brown sugar
4 eggs, beaten
5ml/1 tsp vanilla extract
2.5ml/½ tsp almond extract
115g/4oz/1 cup self-raising
   (self-rising) flour
15ml/1 tbsp unsweetened
   cocoa powder
115g/4oz/⅔ cup walnuts, chopped

1 Preheat the oven to 180°C/350°F/ Gas 4. Lightly grease the cups of a muffin tin (pan) or line them with paper cases.

2 Melt the butter with the chocolate in a heatproof bowl set over a pan of gently simmering water.

3 Stir the sugars into the chocolate mixture. Mix in the eggs, then add the vanilla and almond extracts.

4 Sift over the flour and cocoa. Fold in gently along with the walnuts.

5 Fill the prepared cups and bake until a skewer inserted in the centre comes out clean, 30–35 minutes. Let stand for 5 minutes before turning out on to a rack to cool completely.

Energy 374kcal/1563kJ; Protein 4.9g; Carbohydrate 37.1g, of which sugars 32.2g; Fat 24g, of which saturates 10.8g; Cholesterol 95mg; Calcium 46mg; Fibre 0.8g; Sodium 115mg.

Coffee and macadamia muffins

These creamy and crunchy muffins are good eaten cold, but are best served still warm from the oven. For the ultimate indulgence, serve them freshly baked with a strong black espresso or with a long glass of cold milk.

MAKES 12 STANDARD MUFFINS

25ml/1½ tbsp ground coffee
250ml/8fl oz/1 cup milk
50g/2oz/ ¼ cup butter
275g/10oz/2½ cups plain
  (all-purpose) flour
10ml/2 tsp baking powder
150g/5oz/generous ½ cup light
  muscovado (brown) sugar
75g/3oz/generous ½ cup
  macadamia nuts
1 egg, lightly beaten

1 Preheat the oven to 200°C/400°F/ Gas 6. Lightly grease the cups of a muffin tin (pan) or line them with paper cases.

2 Put the ground coffee in a jug (pitcher). Heat the milk to near-boiling and pour it over. Leave to infuse for 4 minutes, then strain into a mixing bowl. Discard the coffee grounds.

3 Add the butter to the coffee milk and stir until melted. Set aside and leave to cool.

4 Sift the flour and baking powder into a large mixing bowl.

5 Stir the sugar and macadamia nuts into the flour mixture. Make a well in the centre.

6 Add the egg to the coffee-flavoured milk mixture, pour into the dry ingredients and stir until just combined – do not overmix.

7 Divide the batter between the prepared paper cases and bake for about 15 minutes until well risen and firm.

8 Transfer to a wire rack. The muffins will keep for up to three days in an airtight container.

Energy 221kcal/929kJ; Protein 4g; Carbohydrate 32.2g, of which sugars 14.7g; Fat 9.4g, of which saturates 3.3g; Cholesterol 26mg; Calcium 70mg; Fibre 1g; Sodium 59mg.

Double chocolate muffins

These jumbo white and plain chocolate muffins are not for everyday eating, so make them to share with friends. Eat fresh from the oven, while the chocolate chunks are still soft and gooey inside, and the muffins will melt in your mouth. Will keep for three days in an airtight container.

3 In a separate bowl, beat the eggs with the sour cream, milk and oil, then stir into the well in the dry ingredients. Fold in gently, gradually incorporating all the surrounding flour mixture to make a thick and creamy batter.

4 Stir the white and plain chocolate pieces into the batter until just combined.

5 Spoon the batter into the greased muffin tin, filling the cups almost to the top.

6 Bake the muffins for 25–30 minutes, until well risen and firm to the touch. Leave to stand in the tin for a few minutes, then serve warm or turn out on to a wire rack to go completely cold.

MAKES 16 LARGE MUFFINS

400g/14oz/3½ cups plain (all-purpose) flour
15ml/1 tbsp baking powder
30ml/2 tbsp unsweetened cocoa powder
115g/4oz/½ cup muscovado (molasses) sugar
2 eggs
150ml/¼ pint/⅔ cup sour cream
150ml/¼ pint/⅔ cup milk
60ml/4 tbsp sunflower oil
175g/6oz white chocolate, chopped into small pieces
175g/6oz plain (semisweet) chocolate, chopped into pieces

1 Preheat the oven to 180°C/350°F/ Gas 4. Lightly grease the cups of a muffin tin (pan).

2 Sift the flour, baking powder and cocoa into a bowl and stir in the sugar. Make a well in the centre.

Energy 281kcal/1183kJ; Protein 4.7g; Carbohydrate 41.3g, of which sugars 21.9g; Fat 11.9g, of which saturates 5.7g; Cholesterol 7mg; Calcium 94mg; Fibre 1.3g; Sodium 40mg.

Banoffee muffins with caramel

Banoffee pie was invented in the 1980s and immediately became famous. It's a sweet confection that uses *dulce de leche* made by boiling cans of condensed milk for several hours. The addition of coffee to the frosting helps to balance the sweetness. Store in the refrigerator for two days.

MAKES 8–9 LARGE MUFFINS

75g/3oz/6 tbsp butter, softened
115g/4oz/generous ½ cup soft light
   brown sugar
1 egg, lightly beaten
225g/8oz/2 cups self-raising
   (self-rising) flour
12.5ml/2½ tsp baking powder
2 large bananas
rind of 1 orange, finely grated
rind of ½ lemon, finely grated
30ml/2 tbsp buttermilk or
   sour cream
45ml/3 tbsp *dulce de leche*

For the frosting
2.5ml/½ tsp instant coffee granules,
   dissolved in 5ml/1 tsp hot water
150ml/¼ pint/⅔ cup double
   (heavy) cream
7.5ml/1½ tsp *dulce de leche*
½ banana, sliced into 18 discs

For the toffee syrup
10ml/2 tsp dark muscovado
   (molasses) sugar
30ml/2 tbsp *dulce de leche*

1 Preheat the oven to 190°C/375°F/ Gas 5. Lightly grease the cups of a muffin tin (pan).

2 In a large bowl, beat the butter and sugar until creamy. Gradually add the egg.

3 Sift the flour and baking powder into a separate bowl and set aside.

4 Mash the bananas and fold half into the butter–sugar mixture.

5 Add the grated rinds and half of the flour. Fold in the remaining flour and bananas with the buttermilk or sour cream, until just combined.

6 Spoon the batter into the muffin cups until three-quarters full. Bake for 20 minutes until golden and springy to the touch. Let stand for 5 minutes, then turn out on to a rack and leave to cool completely.

7 Make a cavity in the top of each muffin. Fill with *dulce de leche*.

8 To make the frosting, beat together the coffee, cream and *dulce de leche* and beat well. Spread over the cakes. Top with the banana slices.

9 For the syrup, dissolve the sugar in 5ml/1 tsp boiling water. Add the *dulce de leche*. Drizzle over the cakes. Serve immediately or chill.

Energy 341kcal/1432kJ; Protein 4g; Carbohydrate 45.5g, of which sugars 26g; Fat 18.1g, of which saturates 10.6g; Cholesterol 82mg; Calcium 64mg; Fibre 1g; Sodium 79mg.

Blackcurrant muffins with scarlet frosting

Part-cooking the blackcurrants in sugar and redcurrant jelly adds a pleasant tart-sweet flavour to the fruit. The warm syrupy juices left over from the cooked fruit are combined with icing sugar to make a luscious crimson frosting to spread over the tops of the muffins.

MAKES 9–10 STANDARD MUFFINS

75g/3oz/scant ½ cup caster (superfine) sugar
30ml/2 tbsp redcurrant jelly
25g/1oz/2 tbsp butter
225g/8oz/2 cups blackcurrants, topped and tailed, plus extra to decorate
225g/8oz/2 cups plain (all-purpose) flour
12.5ml/2½ tsp baking powder
150g/5oz/scant ¾ cup golden caster (superfine) sugar
75g/3oz/6 tbsp butter, melted
1 egg, lightly beaten
200ml/7fl oz/scant 1 cup buttermilk and milk mixed in equal quantities
5ml/1 tsp grated orange rind
icing (confectioners') sugar

1 Preheat the oven to 190°C/375°F/Gas 5. Line the cups of a muffin tin (pan) with paper cases.

2 To prepare the fruit, dissolve the first three ingredients into a syrup, in a small pan, over a low heat.

3 Set aside the blackcurrants for decoration. Put the rest in a baking tin (pan) and pour the syrup over.

4 Bake for 8 minutes, stirring once. Set aside to cool. Turn the oven temperature down to 180°C/350°F/Gas 4.

5 Sift the flour, baking powder and sugar into a large bowl. Make a well in the centre. Add the butter, egg, buttermilk mixture and orange rind. Fold in until partly blended.

6 Blend the cooled fruit into the batter, reserving the syrup. Three-quarters fill the paper cases and bake for 22–25 minutes. Turn out on to a wire rack and leave to cool.

7 Mix the reserved syrup with enough icing sugar to make a soft frosting. Swirl the frosting over the cooled muffins. Add a few extra berries and serve immediately.

Energy 208kcal/875kJ; Protein 3.7g; Carbohydrate 29.9g, of which sugars 12.7g; Fat 9.1g, of which saturates 5.6g; Cholesterol 43mg; Calcium 78mg; Fibre 1.5g; Sodium 95mg.

Double apricot and amaretto muffins

Amaretto has a special affinity with apricots (both fresh and dried ones are used here), and although it is an expensive addition, the scent alone makes it worthwhile. A glass of milk or an espresso is the ideal accompaniment to these Italian-style muffins. Best served fresh.

MAKES 8–9 STANDARD MUFFINS

225g/8oz/1 cup plain
   (all-purpose) flour
12.5ml/2½ tsp baking powder
2.5ml/½ tsp ground cinnamon
115g/4oz/½ cup caster
   (superfine) sugar
75g/3oz/6 tbsp butter, melted
1 egg, beaten
150ml/¼ pint/⅔ cup buttermilk
a handful ready-to-eat dried
   apricots, cut into strips
2–3 amaretti, crumbled

For the fruit and glaze
275g/10oz fresh apricots
15ml/1 tbsp apricot jam
15ml/1 tbsp clear honey
30ml/2 tbsp amaretto liqueur

1 Preheat the oven to 200°C/400°F/Gas 6. Lightly grease the cups of a muffin tin (pan) or line them with paper cases.

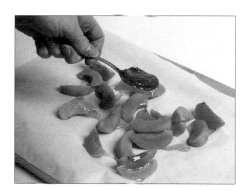

2 To cook the fruit, pit the apricots, cut into quarters and put on a baking tray. Add the apricot jam and honey. Bake for 5 minutes, basting once. Drizzle with the amaretto. Leave to cool.

3 Reduce the oven temperature to 180°C/350°F/Gas 4. Sift the dry ingredients into a large bowl.

4 Mix the butter with the egg and buttermilk. Pour into the dry ingredients and part blend. Add the apricots, reserving the syrup.

5 Spoon the batter into the paper cases. Bake for 28 minutes, until well risen and firm to the touch.

6 Decorate the tops with the dried apricot strips and crumbled amaretti. Return to the oven for 4–5 minutes until the tops look golden. Leave to cool slightly.

7 Heat the reserved syrup in a small pan for 30 seconds, then brush the hot glaze on top of the muffins. When the cakes are cool enough to handle transfer them to a wire rack to go cold.

Energy 216kcal/909kJ; Protein 3.8g; Carbohydrate 34.5g, of which sugars 15g; Fat 7.9g, of which saturates 4.8g; Cholesterol 41mg; Calcium 68mg; Fibre 0.8g; Sodium 84mg.

Chocolate truffle muffins

Not an everyday muffin, these luscious chocolate treats with a hidden truffle centre and equally sinful soft chocolate frosting are decorated with pretty seashell chocolates. The chocolates can be bought or you could make your own using plastic moulds. Eat fresh.

3 Scoop the cool mixture into 9 balls.

4 To make the muffins, in a bowl, beat the butter and sugar. Beat in the eggs. Sift in the flour, cocoa and baking powder and mix lightly.

MAKES 9 STANDARD MUFFINS

165g/5½oz/scant ¾ cup
  butter, softened
150g/5oz/⅔ cup light muscovado
  (brown) sugar
3 eggs, lightly beaten
150g/5oz self-raising
  (self-rising) flour
25g/1oz/¼ cup unsweetened
  cocoa powder
7.5ml/1½ tsp baking powder

For the truffles
150g/5oz dark (bittersweet)
  chocolate, broken into pieces
20ml/4 tsp double (heavy) cream
20ml/4 tsp brandy (optional)

For the frosting
250ml/8fl oz/1 cup double
  (heavy) cream
75g/3oz/⅓ cup soft light brown
  sugar
5ml/1 tsp vanilla extract
150g/5oz dark (bittersweet)
  chocolate, grated

1 Preheat the oven to 180°C/350°F/ Gas 4. Line the cups of a muffin tin (pan) with paper cases.

2 Melt the chocolate in a heatproof bowl set over a pan of simmering water. Remove from the heat, and stir in the cream and the alcohol. Set aside to cool and thicken.

5 Half fill the paper cases. Add a truffle to the centre. Spoon the remaining cake batter on top.

6 Bake for 22–25 minutes or until risen and springy to the touch. Cool.

7 For the frosting, put the cream, sugar and vanilla in a pan and heat until it reaches boiling point. Remove from the heat. Stir in the chocolate until melted. Cool.

8 Spread on top of cold muffins and decorate with chocolate seashells.

Energy 331kcal/1381kJ; Protein 3.6g; Carbohydrate 28.6g, of which sugars 27.4g; Fat 23.5g, of which saturates 14.3g; Cholesterol 110mg; Calcium 32mg; Fibre 0.3g; Sodium 191mg.

Coffee muffins with toffee fudge frosting

With a dense texture and complex flavours these coffee muffins are truly a cake to savour.
The rich and sweet smooth toffee frosting is a contrast to the grainy textured cake. The candy-coated coffee beans add a bittersweet taste. Store for up to three days in an airtight container.

MAKES 10 STANDARD MUFFINS

100ml/3½fl oz/scant ½ cup single
  (light) cream
10ml/2 tsp instant coffee granules
15ml/1 tbsp fine-ground
  roasted coffee
175g/6oz/¾ cup butter, softened
175g/6oz/¾ cup soft light
  brown sugar
2 eggs
100g/3¾oz/scant 1 cup spelt flour
100g/3¾oz/scant 1 cup self-raising
  (self-rising) flour

For the frosting
75g/3oz/6 tbsp butter
75g/3oz/scant ½ cup light
  muscovado (brown) sugar
15ml/1 tbsp golden (light corn)
  syrup
5ml/1 tsp instant coffee granules
130g/4½oz/generous 1 cup icing
  (confectioners') sugar, sifted
5ml/1 tsp lemon juice
candy-coated coffee beans,
  to decorate

1 Place the cream, instant and ground coffees in a small pan and bring to the boil. Remove from the heat. Set aside to cool.

2 Preheat the oven to 180°C/350°F/Gas 4. Line the cups of a muffin tin (pan) with paper cases.

3 In a mixing bowl, beat the butter and sugar until light and creamy, then gradually beat in the eggs one at a time. Beat in the cooled coffee mixture until just combined.

4 Sift the two flours into the creamed mixture and fold in until just combined. Do not overmix.

5 Three-quarters fill the paper cases with the batter. Bake for 20–25 minutes. Leave to stand for 5 minutes in the tin before turning out on to a wire rack to go completely cold.

6 To make the frosting, melt 50g/2oz/¼ cup of the butter with the sugar and golden syrup in a pan over a low heat, stirring occasionally.

7 Dissolve the coffee in 50ml/2fl oz/¼ cup boiling water and add to the ingredients in the pan. Bring slowly to the boil, stirring frequently, then simmer for 3 minutes, stirring once or twice. Remove from the heat and pour into a large bowl.

8 Whisk in the icing sugar, then the lemon juice and remaining butter. Beat until smooth. Stand the bowl in iced water and stir until the mixture thickens. Spread on to the tops of the muffins. Decorate with candy-coated coffee beans.

Energy 441kcal/1846kJ; Protein 3.6g; Carbohydrate 56.7g, of which sugars 41.5g; Fat 23.8g, of which saturates 15.1g; Cholesterol 101mg; Calcium 56mg; Fibre 1.5g; Sodium 213mg.

Halloween muffins with spooky frosting

No wonder kids love Halloween when there are treats like these to be enjoyed. These dark spicy muffins are very moist and make good use of the pumpkin flesh from the Jack-o-lanterns. Make them in advance if you can (without the topping), as the flavour will improve after a few days.

MAKES 10 STANDARD MUFFINS

100ml/3½fl oz/scant ½ cup olive oil
175g/6oz/¾ cup light muscovado (brown) sugar
50g/2oz/¼ cup soft dark brown sugar
1 egg, lightly beaten
7.5ml/1½ tsp vanilla extract
275g/10oz pumpkin flesh, grated
175g/6oz sultanas (golden raisins)
275g/10oz/2½ cups self-raising (self-rising) flour, sifted
10ml/2 tsp mixed (apple pie) spice
5ml/1 tsp ground ginger

For the ginger frosting and decorations
250g/9oz/2¼ cups icing (confectioners') sugar, sifted
5ml/1 tsp ground ginger
15ml/1 tbsp lemon juice
30ml/2 tbsp ginger syrup from a jar of preserved stem ginger
175g/6oz white sugarpaste (fondant icing)
mini marshmallows

1 Preheat the oven to 180°C/350°F/ Gas 4. Line the cups of a muffin tin (pan) with paper cases.

2 In a large bowl, beat the oil with the sugars. Add the egg and beat well. Stir in the vanilla extract, grated pumpkin and sultanas.

3 Sift the flour and spices into the batter and stir until just mixed.

4 Divide the batter between the paper cases. Bake for 28 minutes, or until risen and golden. Leave to set. Turn out on to a wire rack to go cold.

5 To make the ginger frosting, mix the first four ingredients together in a large bowl, then spoon over the tops of the cakes and leave to set.

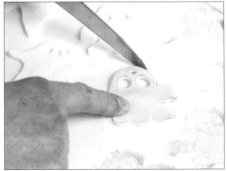

6 Roll out the sugarpaste and cut out Halloween decorations. Stick them to the tops of the muffins. Serve sprinkled with marshmallows.

Energy 405kcal/1718kJ; Protein 4g; Carbohydrate 85.6g, of which sugars 65g; Fat 7.6g, of which saturates 1.2g; Cholesterol 19mg; Calcium 144mg; Fibre 1.5g; Sodium 120mg.

Kids' chocolate party muffins

A generous covering of bright and colourful sweets, sprinkles and marshmallows over a thick chocolate frosting is bound to go down well with children of all ages. Children will love to help decorate these luscious chocolate muffins. Will keep for up to three days in the refrigerator.

MAKES 9–10 STANDARD MUFFINS

165g/5½oz/scant ¾ cup butter, softened
150g/5oz/¾ cup caster (superfine) sugar
5ml/1 tsp vanilla extract
150g/5oz/1¼ cups self-raising (self-rising) flour
20g/¾oz/scant ¼ cup unsweetened cocoa powder
7.5ml/1½ tsp baking powder
3 eggs, beaten
50–60 small sweets (candies)
coloured sprinkles

For the frosting
250ml/8fl oz/1 cup crème fraîche
225g/8oz plain (semisweet) chocolate, broken into pieces
75g/3oz/¾ cup icing (confectioners') sugar

1 Preheat the oven to 180°C/350°F/Gas 4. Lightly grease the cups of a muffin tin (pan) or line them with paper cases.

2 In a large bowl, beat together the butter, sugar and vanilla until light and creamy.

3 Sift the flour, cocoa and baking powder into the butter and sugar mixture and beat to combine. Add the eggs and beat well.

4 Divide the batter between the paper cases and bake for 22–25 minutes or until risen and springy to the touch. Leave to stand for a few minutes then turn out on to a wire rack to go cold.

5 To make the frosting, heat the crème fraîche over a low heat until hot, but not boiling. Remove from the heat.

6 Add the chocolate and stir until melted. Sift in the icing sugar and mix until smooth. Set aside to thicken slightly. Spread in swirls over the muffins.

7 Decorate with confectionery.

Energy 392kcal/1641kJ; Protein 5g; Carbohydrate 42.2g, of which sugars 30.5g; Fat 23.8g, of which saturates 14.8g; Cholesterol 111mg; Calcium 110mg; Fibre 0.7g; Sodium 235mg.

Raspberry and white chocolate muffins

White chocolate and fresh raspberries are a combination that work particularly well in muffins. Serve them warm and freshly baked. For a special occasion add a white chocolate truffle to the batter before baking. It's a rich addition, so you could make some without. Eat fresh.

MAKES 8 LARGE MUFFINS

225g/8oz/2 cups plain
  (all-purpose) flour
15ml/1 tbsp baking powder
115g/4oz/generous ½ cup caster
  (superfine) sugar
20g/¾oz/scant ¼ cup ground
  almonds
50g/2oz white, or white vanilla
  chocolate, chopped into nibs
2 eggs, beaten
75g/3oz/scant ½ cup butter, melted
50ml/2fl oz/¼ cup vegetable oil
30ml/2 tbsp milk
150g/5oz/scant 1 cup raspberries

For the chocolate truffles
150ml/¼ pint/⅔ cup double
  (heavy) cream
5ml/1 tsp finely grated orange rind
350g/12oz white chocolate
50g/2oz/¼ cup butter
icing (confectioners') sugar

1 To make the truffles, in a pan, bring the cream to the boil. Stir in the orange rind, then leave to cool for 1–2 minutes.

2 Add the white chocolate. Stir constantly until it melts.

3 Add the butter and continue to stir until smooth and glossy. Cool over a bowl of iced water, stirring frequently until the mixture begins to thicken (15–30 minutes).

4 Using a teaspoon, scoop 8 balls of the ganache on to a baking sheet lined with silicone paper. Chill for 1–2 hours until set.

5 Lightly dust your fingers with icing sugar and roll the ganache into balls. Chill again until firm. Store the truffles in the refrigerator layered between sheets of silicone paper in an airtight container. The truffles will keep for up to 1 week.

6 Preheat the oven to 180°C/350°F/ Gas 4. Lightly grease the cups of a muffin tin (pan) or line them with paper cases.

7 Sift the flour, baking powder and sugar into a large bowl. Stir in the ground almonds and the chocolate.

8 In a jug (pitcher), mix together the eggs, butter and oil. Pour into the dry ingredients and fold lightly in with the milk until partly combined.

9 Gently fold in the raspberries.

10 Divide half of the batter between the paper cases. Press a truffle into each. Fill with the remaining batter.

11 Bake for 25 minutes, until the muffins are well risen and springy to the touch. Leave to stand for a few minutes, then turn out on to a wire rack to cool completely.

Energy 694kcal/2896kJ; Protein 9.6g; Carbohydrate 67.8g, of which sugars 46.3g; Fat 45.7g, of which saturates 24.2g; Cholesterol 108mg; Calcium 216mg; Fibre 1.5g; Sodium 201mg.

Savoury muffins

Perfect for serving for lunch with soup, or instead of savoury crackers with pâté or cheese, this delicious collection of muffin recipes is guaranteed to please. As well as the more traditional flavours of mature Cheddar, chilli and cheese, and corn muffins with ham, there are unusual recipes for bacon, Brie and fresh date muffins, wild mushrooms and mace, and broccoli and blue cheese. All are perfect for eating as a between-meals snack, to accompany a meal, or as a brunch-time treat on their own.

Shallot, thyme and garlic cheese muffins

These light muffins are best served warm, fresh from the oven, when the cream cheese and the caramelized flavour complement each other perfectly. Spread them with soft cheese for a mid-morning snack with a strong cup of coffee, or serve with soup, for lunch.

MAKES 10 TALL MUFFINS

225g/8oz shallots, peeled
25ml/1½ tbsp olive oil, for frying
15g/½oz/1 tbsp unsalted butter,
  for frying
10ml/2 tsp fresh thyme, plus a few
  sprigs for decoration
salt and ground black pepper
225g/8oz/2 cups self-raising
  (self-rising) flour
pinch of salt
10ml/2 tsp baking powder
10ml/2 tsp caster (superfine) sugar
115g/4oz soft herb and garlic
  cream cheese
175ml/6fl oz/¾ cup milk
2 eggs
75g/3oz/6 tbsp butter, melted

1 Preheat the oven to 180°C/ 350°F/Gas 4. Lightly grease and line 10 dariole moulds with baking parchment.

2 Drop the peeled shallots into a pan of boiling water and blanch them for 2 minutes. Drain thoroughly, then leave to stand on kitchen paper. When the shallots are cool enough to handle, slice them into quarters.

3 In a frying pan, heat the oil and butter over a medium heat. Add the shallots and sauté them, until caramelized on all sides. Stir in the thyme and seasoning. Leave to cool.

4 In a large bowl, sift together the flour, salt, baking powder and sugar.

5 In another bowl, beat together the cream cheese, milk, eggs and melted butter. Pour into a well in the centre of the dry ingredients and blend until partly mixed.

6 Scrape the shallots and any liquid into the batter (reserving a few of them for decorating) and stir lightly.

7 Divide the batter between the moulds and dot with the reserved shallots and a few thyme sprigs.

8 Bake for 25–30 minutes or until the tops are firm to the touch. Leave to cool slightly then invert on to a floured tray. Serve warm.

Energy 236kcal/984kJ; Protein 4.5g; Carbohydrate 20.7g, of which sugars 3.5g; Fat 15.6g, of which saturates 9g; Cholesterol 71mg; Calcium 124mg; Fibre 1g; Sodium 207mg.

Chilli cheese muffins

Prepare for a whole new taste sensation with these fabulous spicy muffins – they're hot stuff. Sharp cheese, aromatic garlic and the heat of the chilli purée combine in a muffin that is light but filling, with a grainy texture. Serve fresh with soup.

MAKES 12 STANDARD MUFFINS

115g/4oz/1 cup self-raising (self-rising) flour
15ml/1 tbsp baking powder
225g/8oz/2 cups fine cornmeal (polenta)
150g/5oz/1¼ cups grated mature (sharp) Cheddar cheese
50g/2oz/¼ cup butter, melted
2 eggs, beaten
5ml/1 tsp chilli purée (paste)
1 garlic clove, crushed
300ml/½ pint/1¼ cups milk

1 Preheat the oven to 200°C/400°F/Gas 6. Line the cups of a muffin tin (pan) with paper cases.

3 In a small bowl, stir together the melted butter, eggs, chilli purée, crushed garlic and milk until thoroughly combined.

4 Pour the liquid on to the dry ingredients and mix quickly until just combined.

5 Spoon the batter into the prepared paper cases and sprinkle the remaining grated cheese on top.

6 Bake for about 20 minutes, until risen and golden. Leave to cool for a few minutes before transferring to a wire rack to go cold, or serve warm.

2 Sift the flour and baking powder together into a bowl, then stir in the cornmeal and 115g/4oz/1 cup of the grated cheese until well mixed.

Energy 166kcal/698kJ; Protein 5.1g; Carbohydrate 19.3g, of which sugars 4.4g; Fat 8.1g, of which saturates 4.6g; Cholesterol 60mg; Calcium 93mg; Fibre 0.6g; Sodium 96mg.

Savoury cheese muffins

Puffed up and golden with their yummy cheese filling and the merest hint of hot spice, these must top the list of everyone's favourite savoury muffins. Serve them warm and freshly baked, to accompany a hearty soup in winter or a lunchtime salad. Store for up to three days.

MAKES 9 STANDARD MUFFINS

175g/6oz/1½ cups plain
  (all-purpose) flour
10ml/2 tsp baking powder
30ml/2 tbsp caster (superfine)
  sugar
5ml/1 tsp paprika
2 eggs
120ml/4fl oz/½ cup milk
50g/2oz/¼ cup butter, melted
5ml/1 tsp dried thyme
50g/2oz mature (sharp) Cheddar
  cheese, diced

1 Preheat the oven to 190°C/375°F/ Gas 5. Lightly grease the cups of a muffin tin (pan) or line them with paper cases.

2 Sift together the flour, baking powder, caster sugar and paprika into a large bowl. Make a well in the centre. Set aside.

3 Combine the eggs, milk, melted butter and dried thyme in another bowl and beat lightly with a whisk until thoroughly blended.

4 Add the milk mixture to the dry ingredients and stir lightly with a wooden spoon until just combined. Do not overmix.

5 Place a heaped tablespoonful of the mixture in each of the prepared paper cases.

6 Divide the pieces of cheese equally among the paper cases.

7 Top with another spoonful of the batter, ensuring that the cheese is covered.

8 Bake for about 25 minutes, until puffed and golden. Leave to stand for 5 minutes before transferring to a wire rack to cool slightly. These muffins are best served while they are still warm.

Energy 166kcal/698kJ; Protein 5.1g; Carbohydrate 19.3g, of which sugars 4.4g; Fat 8.1g, of which saturates 4.6g; Cholesterol 60mg; Calcium 93mg; Fibre 0.6g; Sodium 96mg.

Corn muffins with ham

These delicious little muffins are perfect to serve as an appetizer with hot soup. If you like, serve them unfilled with a pot of herb butter. The batter will make half the number of standard muffins, if you prefer. Serve them cold and freshly baked.

MAKES 24 MINI MUFFINS

50g/2oz/scant ½ cup yellow
  cornmeal (polenta)
65g/2½oz/generous ½ cup plain
  (all-purpose) flour, sifted
30ml/2 tbsp caster (superfine) sugar
7.5ml/1½ tsp baking powder
50g/2oz/¼ cup butter, melted
120ml/4fl oz/½ cup
  whipping cream
1 egg
1–2 jalapeño or other medium-hot
  chillies, seeded and finely
  chopped (optional)
pinch of cayenne pepper
butter, for spreading
grainy mustard or mustard with
  honey, for spreading
50g/2oz oak-smoked ham, sliced,
  for filling

1 Preheat the oven to 200°C/400°F/
Gas 6.

2 Lightly grease the cups of a mini muffin tin (pan) or line them with mini paper cases.

3 In a large bowl, combine the cornmeal, sifted flour, sugar and baking powder.

4 In another bowl, whisk together the melted butter, cream, egg, chopped chillies, if using, and the cayenne pepper.

5 Make a well in the cornmeal mixture, pour in the egg mixture and gently stir in just enough to blend (do not over-beat – the batter does not have to be smooth).

6 Drop a spoonful of batter into each paper case. Bake for 12–15 minutes, until golden. Leave to stand for a few minutes in the tin, then transfer to a wire rack to go completely cold.

7 Split the muffins, spread with a little butter and mustard and sandwich together with ham.

Energy 54kcal/227kJ; Protein 1.5g; Carbohydrate 6.8g, of which sugars 1.6g; Fat 2.5g, of which saturates 1.4g; Cholesterol 14mg; Calcium 13mg; Fibre 0.2g; Sodium 43mg.

Bacon, Brie and fresh date muffins

The strong flavours of bacon and fresh dates make a wonderful marriage. With the addition of Brie, these little muffins are delicious and unusual enough to serve in miniature form as tempting canapés with pre-dinner drinks. The batter will make 12–14 standard muffins, if you prefer

5 When it is cool enough to handle, cut the warm bacon into small pieces and stir it back into the warm juices in the pan. Cover with foil and set aside.

MAKES 24–28 MINI MUFFINS

225g/8oz/2 cups plain
  (all-purpose) flour
pinch of salt
10ml/2 tsp baking powder
10ml/2 tsp caster (superfine) sugar
12 fresh dates, pitted
30ml/2 tbsp olive oil, for frying
15g/½oz/1 tbsp butter, for frying
12 rashers (strips) smoked, streaky
  (fatty) bacon
75g/3oz Brie, diced
150ml/¼ pint/⅔ cup milk
50g/2oz/¼ cup butter, melted
2 eggs, beaten

1 Preheat the oven to 180°C/350°F/ Gas 5. Lightly grease the cups of a mini muffin tin (pan) or line them with mini paper cases.

2 In a large bowl, sift together the flour, salt, baking powder and sugar and set aside.

3 Using a knife dusted with flour, chop the dates into small pieces. Separate out any small clumps and add to the flour mixture.

4 In a frying pan, heat the oil and butter over a medium heat, and fry the bacon until crisp, 4 minutes.

6 Mash the Brie as finely as you can into the milk, then mix it into the dry ingredients along with the melted butter, eggs, the fried bacon and any juices from the pan. Mix lightly together until just combined.

7 Fill the prepared paper cases three-quarters full. Bake for 18–20 minutes, until risen and golden.

8 Leave to stand and set for five minutes before turning out on to a wire rack. Serve warm, or store for up to 3 days in an airtight container. Warm in a microwave.

Energy 183kcal/724kJ; Protein 4.9g; Carbohydrate 12.2g, of which sugars 0.6g; Fat 11.9.6g, of which saturates 8.3g; Cholesterol 53mg; Calcium 99mg; Fibre 0.8g; Sodium 202mg.

Vegetable muffins

Onions, courgettes, cream cheese and herbs have a healthy appeal. When combined in these vegetarian muffins, they have a sharp and tangy flavour and a moist texture. Serve them warm to accompany a light summer salad. Keep for up to two days in an airtight container.

MAKES 8 TALL MUFFINS

150g/5oz courgettes (zucchini)
250g/9oz/2¼ cups self-raising
   (self-rising) flour
pinch of celery salt or salt
12.5ml/2½ tsp baking powder
5ml/1 tsp caster (superfine) sugar
3.5ml/¾ tsp cayenne pepper
8 spring onions (scallions)
30ml/2 tbsp red onion, grated
10ml/2 tsp malt vinegar
ground black pepper
115g/4oz/1 cup soft herb and
   cream cheese
60ml/4 tbsp sour cream
75g/3oz/6 tbsp butter, melted
2 eggs
15ml/1 tbsp mixed fresh parsley
   and thyme, finely chopped
15g/½oz Parmesan cheese
1 small courgette (zucchini),
   to decorate
olive oil, to drizzle

1 Preheat the oven to 180°C/ 350°F/Gas 4. Lightly grease and line 8 dariole moulds with baking parchment.

2 Coarsely grate the courgettes into a bowl.

3 In a large bowl, sift together the flour, salt, baking powder, sugar and cayenne pepper and set aside.

4 Slice the white parts of the spring onions into thin discs and add to the courgettes with the grated red onion. Sprinkle with the vinegar. Season and set aside to marinate.

5 In a small bowl, whisk the cheese into the sour cream, then whisk in the melted butter, eggs and herbs.

6 Pour into the dry ingredients with the Parmesan and grated vegetables and any juices from the bowl. Stir to mix until just combined.

7 Fill the prepared paper cases three-quarters full, and decorate each with 4 thin slices of courgette cut at a 45 degree angle, if you like. Drizzle lightly with olive oil. Add a few twists of black pepper and bake for 25–30 minutes.

8 Leave to cool slightly, then transfer to a wire rack to go cold.

Energy 291kcal/1215kJ; Protein 6.8g; Carbohydrate 25.8g, of which sugars 1.9g; Fat 18.6g, of which saturates 11.1g; Cholesterol 126mg; Calcium 109mg; Fibre 1.4g; Sodium 154mg.

Walnut, cheese and barleycorn muffins

This recipe uses a mixture of self-raising and barleycorn flour, which contains mixed grains that provide texture as well as flavour. Chopped walnuts add extra crunch. Serve warm, mid-morning with a cup of coffee, or for a more substantial snack, add a slice of cheese and a crisp apple.

MAKES 8 STANDARD MUFFINS

115g/4oz/1 cup self-raising (self-rising) flour
10ml/2 tsp baking powder
3.5ml/¾ tsp cayenne pepper
150g/5oz/1¼ cups barleycorn bread flour
150g/5oz/1¼ cups mature (sharp) Cheddar cheese, grated
2 eggs
50ml/2fl oz/¼ cup milk
100ml/3½fl oz/scant ½ cup buttermilk
3.5ml/¾ tsp English mustard
75g/3oz/6 tbsp butter, melted
30ml/2 tbsp finely chopped fresh parsley
25g/1oz/1½ tbsp walnuts, chopped

1 Preheat the oven to 190°C/375°F/ Gas 5. Lightly grease the cups of a muffin tin (pan), or line them with paper cases.

2 Sift the flour, baking powder, salt and cayenne into a mixing bowl. Stir in the barleycorn flour with the grated cheese until well combined.

3 In a small bowl, whisk the eggs, milk, buttermilk and mustard together. Mix in the melted butter.

4 Pour the liquid into the dry ingredients with the parsley. Fold in until half blended, then fold in the chopped walnuts.

5 Divide the batter equally between the paper cases and bake for 25 minutes, until golden on top and springy to the touch.

6 Leave in the tin for 5 minutes, then turn out on to a wire rack.

> **VARIATION**
> Use self-raising (self-rising) flour, in place of barleycorn flour.

Energy 291kcal/1216kJ; Protein 9g; Carbohydrate 26.4g, of which sugars 1.6g; Fat 16.9g, of which saturates 9.6g; Cholesterol 41mg; Calcium 233mg; Fibre 2.8g; Sodium 272mg.

Bacon, mushroom and maple syrup muffins

These delicious muffins make the perfect treat on Sunday morning. Serve one or two of the freshly baked muffins per person on warmed plates and top with extra hot crispy bacon and a drizzle of warm maple syrup for a special occasion brunch.

MAKES 8–9 LARGE MUFFINS

225g/8oz/2 cups plain
  (all-purpose) flour
12.5ml/2½ tsp baking powder
30ml/2 tbsp olive oil, for frying
25g/1oz/2 tbsp butter, for frying
150g/5oz streaky (fatty) smoked
  bacon rashers (strips)
115g/4oz/1½ cups small flat
  mushrooms, thinly sliced
2 eggs
200ml/7fl oz/scant 1 cup
  buttermilk
75g/3oz/6 tbsp butter, melted
10ml/2 tsp maple syrup
extra rashers (strips) of streaky
  (fatty) bacon and maple syrup,
  to serve

1 Preheat the oven to 180°C/350°F/Gas 5. Lightly grease the cups of a muffin tin (pan).

2 In a large bowl, sift together the flour and baking powder.

3 In a pan, heat the oil and butter and fry the bacon gently until crisp, about 4 minutes. Remove from the heat. Cut into small strips, cover with foil and keep warm.

4 Return the pan to the heat and stir the mushrooms in the hot oil for 30 seconds. Set them aside in the pan.

5 In a small bowl, beat the eggs, buttermilk and melted butter together. Pour the liquid into the dry ingredients with the maple syrup. Stir until partly combined.

6 Add the bacon and mushrooms and any juices from the pan and stir in. Do not overmix.

7 Fill the prepared paper cases and bake for 25 minutes until well risen and firm to the touch. Leave to cool slightly then turn out on to a wire rack to go cool. Serve immediately.

Energy 286kcal/1197kJ; Protein 7.5g; Carbohydrate 29.4g, of which sugars 10.3g; Fat 16.3g, of which saturates 8g; Cholesterol 78mg; Calcium 74mg; Fibre 0.9g; Sodium 399mg.

Broccoli and blue cheese muffins

Stilton, with its distinctive blue veins running through a round of cream-colour cheese, is perfect for these muffins, but you could use any sharp-tasting blue cheese. The creamy texture blends smoothly with the broccoli to add the most divine savoury flavour to these muffins. Serve fresh.

3 In a frying pan, heat the oil and butter over a medium heat, add the broccoli and fry gently for 90 seconds, stirring. Scrape from the pan into a bowl and leave to cool.

4 Sift the flour and baking powder into a large bowl and set aside.

5 In a jug (pitcher), beat together the sour cream, melted butter, milk and eggs. Pour into the dry ingredients and partly combine.

MAKES 8 STANDARD MUFFINS

150g/5oz broccoli
30ml/2 tbsp olive oil, for frying
40g/1½oz/3 tbsp butter, for frying
250g/9oz/2¼ cups self-raising
  (self-rising) flour
12.5ml/2½ tsp baking powder
30ml/2 tbsp sour cream
75g/3oz/6 tbsp butter, melted
45ml/3 tbsp milk
2 eggs
20ml/4 tsp sweet chilli
  dipping sauce
150g/5oz Stilton, such as Colston
  Bassett, grated

1 Preheat the oven to 180°C/350°F/ Gas 4. Line the cups of a muffin tin (pan) with paper cases.

2 Cut the broccoli florets into tiny pieces. Discard the stems.

6 Stir in the broccoli, chilli sauce and Stilton, until just combined.

7 Spoon the batter into the paper cases. Bake for 25 minutes until golden and puffed up. Leave to stand in the tin for a few minutes, then transfer to a wire rack to cool.

Energy 346kcal/1441kJ; Protein 9.8g; Carbohydrate 24.4g, of which sugars 1.1g; Fat 23.6g, of which saturates 13.3g; Cholesterol 103mg; Calcium 199mg; Fibre 1.5g; Sodium 418mg.

Brioche muffins with savoury pâté stuffing

Serve these savoury brioche-style muffins with cold cuts of meat, quiche and salad at a picnic, or for an appetizer with a selection of toasted breads to accompany pâté. These muffins take time to prepare but the results are well worthwhile. Eat fresh, either warm or cold, for the best taste.

MAKES 10 TALL MUFFINS

15g/½oz fresh yeast
4 medium (US large) eggs
350g/12oz/3 cups plain
  (all-purpose) flour
35g/1¼oz/3 tbsp caster (superfine)
  sugar
10g/¼oz salt
175g/6oz/¾ cup unsalted butter,
  softened
150g/5oz fairly coarse pâté
45ml/3 tbsp milk
1 small egg yolk

1 Crumble the yeast into the bottom of the bowl of a food processor, fitted with a dough hook, and mix with 10ml/2 tsp warm water until well blended.

2 Add the eggs, flour, sugar and salt. Beat together at a low speed for 6–7 minutes until a dough forms. Turn up to a moderate speed and gradually add the butter. Continue to knead for 12–15 minutes until the dough is smooth and shiny.

3 Seal the dough in a plastic bag and leave in the refrigerator for 24 hours, or overnight.

4 Line the cups of individual dariole moulds with paper cases.

5 Divide the pâté into 10 pieces, and with lightly floured hands, form them into balls. Set aside.

6 Place the dough on a floured work surface. Form it into a sausage and cut it into 10 equal pieces.

7 Add a ball of pâté to the centre of each piece of dough, then press the dough around the pâté to form a smooth ball. With the seal below, put the dough into the paper cases.

8 Preheat the oven to 220°C/425°F/ Gas 7. In a small bowl, mix the milk and egg yolk together to make an egg wash. Using a pastry brush, apply it thinly over the top of each dough ball. With a sharp knife slash the top of each muffin twice. Leave in a warm place to prove for 15 minutes.

9 Bake for 13–15 minutes, until well risen and golden. Turn out the muffins with a sharp shake on to a floured tray and leave them to cool.

Energy 347kcal/1449kJ; Protein 8.3g; Carbohydrate 31.2g, of which sugars 4.5g; Fat 21.9g, of which saturates 11.6g; Cholesterol 162mg; Calcium 75mg; Fibre 1.1g; Sodium 282mg.

Devils on horseback

The very moreish combination of salty bacon and sweet fresh dates makes an unusual and seductive addition to these light and delicious muffins. These are perfect for any time of day when only a savoury snack will do. Eat fresh for best results.

MAKES 10 STANDARD MUFFINS

225g/8oz/2 cups self-raising (self-rising) flour
10ml/2 tsp baking powder
10ml/2 tsp caster (superfine) sugar
12 rashers (strips) thin-cut smoked, streaky (fatty) bacon
24 fresh dates, pitted
30ml/2 tbsp olive oil, for frying
15g/½oz/1 tbsp butter, for frying
10ml/2 tsp fresh thyme or oregano, plus a few leaves for decoration
115g/4oz/1 cup soft herb and garlic cream cheese
175ml/6fl oz/¾ cup milk
75g/3oz/6 tbsp butter, melted
2 eggs
ground black pepper

1 Preheat the oven to 180°C/350°F/ Gas 5. Line the cups of a muffin tin (pan) with baking parchment.

2 Sift the flour, baking powder and sugar into a mixing bowl.

3 Using scissors, cut each bacon rasher in half and wrap one around each date.

4 In a frying pan, heat the oil and butter over a medium heat, and when it is foaming, add the bacon rolls and sauté them, turning them in the juices until they are crisp and caramelized on all sides, 4 minutes. Stir in the thyme or oregano and season with the pepper. Leave to cool slightly in the warm juices.

5 When cool enough to handle, slice each of the bacon-wrapped dates into 4 discs. Return them to the pan and cover with foil.

6 Beat the cream cheese into the milk, with the butter and eggs. Pour into the dry ingredients and stir lightly until part blended. Scrape the bacon and date slices with any of the cooking juices into the batter and stir until evenly combined. Avoid overmixing.

7 Divide the batter between the paper cases and dot with a few extra thyme leaves. Bake for 25 minutes or until the tops are golden.

8 Leave the muffins to cool slightly then turn out on to a wire rack to cool. Serve warm or cold.

Energy 318kcal/1327kJ; Protein 8g; Carbohydrate 23.6g, of which sugars 6.9g; Fat 22g, of which saturates 11g; Cholesterol 85mg; Calcium 124mg; Fibre 1g; Sodium 491mg.

Wild mushroom and pine nut muffins

These light flavoured savoury muffins make attractive accompaniments to soft cheeses, pâtés and soups. The pine nuts are decorative as well as adding texture and crunch, and a delicious warm nutty flavour. Serve them freshly baked and warm to enjoy them at their best.

MAKES 6–7 LARGE MUFFINS

250g/9oz/2¼ cups self-raising
    (self-rising) flour
11.5ml/2¼ tsp baking powder
150g/5oz mixture of wild
    mushrooms
90g/3½oz/scant ½ cup butter,
    for frying
large pinch cayenne pepper
large pinch mace
50–75g/2–3oz/½–¾ cup pine nuts
30ml/2 tbsp olive oil
90ml/6 tbsp buttermilk
75g/3oz/6 tbsp butter, melted
2 eggs

1 Preheat the oven to 180°C/350°F/ Gas 4. Lightly grease the cups of a muffin tin (pan).

2 In a large bowl, sift the flour and baking powder and set aside.

3 Clean and slice the mushrooms. In a frying pan, heat 75g/3oz/6 tbsp of the butter over a medium heat. When it is foaming, add the mushrooms. Season with cayenne pepper and mace. Fry gently, stirring, until just softened. Scrape into a bowl and set aside to cool.

4 Fry the pine nuts in the remaining butter and the olive oil for 30 seconds. Add to the mushrooms

5 Beat together the buttermilk, melted butter and eggs in a bowl.

6 Stir into the dry ingredients with the mushrooms and pine nuts.

7 Spoon the batter into the muffin tins and bake for 25 minutes until the tops are golden and firm.

Energy 399kcal/1660kJ; Protein 6.9g; Carbohydrate 28g, of which sugars 1.4g; Fat 29.6g, of which saturates 14.2g; Cholesterol 109mg; Calcium 154mg; Fibre 1.5g; Sodium 334mg.

Index

AUTHOR'S ACKNOWLEDGEMENTS

For the Kenwood Chef Titanium
KM010 cake mixer
Kenwood
www.kenwood.co.uk

For lemon squeezer and coffee
percolator
De Longhi
www.delonghi.co.uk

For muffin tins and kitchen items
Lakeland
www.lakeland.co.uk

For sugar
Whitworths sugars
www.whitworth-sugars.com

For organic speciality flours
Doves Farm Foods
www.dovesfarm.co.uk